Close Reading Companion

Mc Graw Hill Education

Cover and Title Page: Nathan Love

www.mheonline.com/readingwonders

Send all inquiries to:
McGraw-Hill Education
Two Penn Plaza
New York, New York 10121

ISBN: 978-0-02-130873-6
MHID: 0-02-130873-X

Printed in the United States of America.

8 9 10 11 12 13 LMN 21 20 19 18 17

C

Think It Through

Amazing Animals

That's the Spirit!

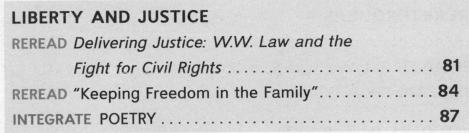

David Frazier/Corbis

v

FACT OR FICTION?

FIGURE IT OUT

James Quine/Alamy

Past, Present, and Future

The Princess and the Pizza

Literature Anthology: pages 10–25

? How does the author help you understand how Paulina's new life is different from her old life?

COLLABORATE

Talk About It Reread the second paragraph on pages 12–13. Turn to a partner and describe what Paulina's life was like before and what it is like now.

Cite Text Evidence How does the author show how Paulina's life has changed? Write evidence in the chart.

Paulina's Old Life	Paulina's New Life	How do you know?

Tip of the Week

When I **reread**, I use text and illustrations to help me understand the characters better.

Write To help me understand how Paulina's life has changed, the author _____

_____

_____

Kyle

KidStock/Blend Images/Getty Images

? **How does Paulina's response to the princess-and-the-pea trick help you understand more about her character?**

COLLABORATE

Talk About It Reread the first paragraph on page 15. Talk with a partner about Paulina's response to the princess-and-the-pea trick. Why is it funny?

Cite Text Evidence What words and phrases show how Paulina responds to the trick? Write text evidence and explain what you learned about her.

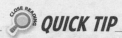
QUICK TIP

When I reread, I can use how the characters respond to help me know more about them.

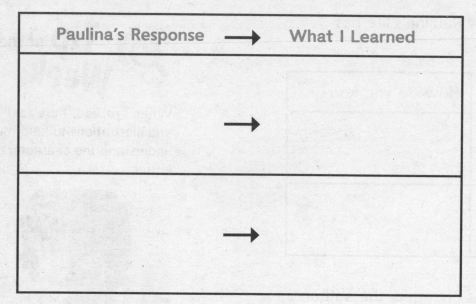

Paulina's Response	⟶	What I Learned
	⟶	
	⟶	

Write Paulina's response to the princess-and-the-pea trick helps me know that

_____

_____

? **How does the author use what the characters say to help you understand how they feel at the end of the fairy tale?**

Talk About It Reread page 24. Turn to a partner and talk about what Paulina and the queen say about how the contest ends.

Cite Text Evidence How do you know how each character feels at the end of the story? Write text evidence in the chart.

How the Characters Feel	What They Say

Write I know how the characters changed because _____

_____

 **QUICK TIP**

I can use these sentence frames when we talk about the contest.

Paulina says that she . . .

The queen tells Paulina that . . .

Your Turn

How does the author show that winning the contest changes Paulina's life? Use these sentence frames to focus your text evidence.

In the beginning, Paulina . . .

Then the author . . .

This shows that Paulina's life . . .

Go Digital!
Write your response online.

Tomás and His Sons

[1]   Hard work was something Tomás knew well. But his sons Eduardo, Miguel, and Luis, were the laziest boys in all of Mexico.

[2]   While their parents tilled the earth under the hot afternoon sun, the boys slept. As the sun bent toward evening, the brothers rose. They stumbled into the kitchen. They filled their plates with eggs and tortillas. By nightfall they were wide awake. Soon, they were off to the village to sing and dance until morning.

[3]   Tomás worried about the land. What would happen once he and his wife, Maria, were too old to work? Their sons showed no interest in the vines. Once, Tomás had asked the boys to walk through the vineyard with him. He again told them about their ancestors bringing the vines from Spain.

[4]   "These vines tell our family's story," Tomás said. But he knew his words were lost on the boys. The farm's success was not as exciting as last night's fiesta.

Reread and use the prompts to take notes in the text.

In paragraph 1, underline how the author describes Tomás. Then circle how he describes Eduardo, Miguel, and Luis.

COLLABORATE

Reread paragraph 2. Talk with a partner about how Tomás and his sons are different.

Underline phrases that tell what Tomás does all day.

Circle phrases that tell what his sons do all day.

What does Tomás worry about? Make marks in the margin beside text evidence. Write it here:

1. _____

2. _____

1. Many happy seasons passed with the family digging together in the vineyard. The sons were amazed each year to see the big, juicy grapes. Even more, they were thrilled by the wealth the crop had brought them.

2. One day, long after the farmer's sons had taken over the vineyard, Luis asked his brothers, "Have we found the great treasure yet?"

3. The three brothers began to laugh. They had forgotten that they were digging to find treasure. Yet all their hard work made them realize that their vineyard was a treasure.

Reread paragraph 1. Underline phrases that show how the sons felt about working in the vineyard. Write them here:

1. _____

2. _____

Reread paragraphs 2 and 3. Circle how you know the brothers had forgotten about the great treasure.

COLLABORATE

Talk with a partner about why they began to laugh. What did they realize?

? **How do you know that the brothers' attitudes have changed about their family's vineyard?**

Talk About It Reread the excerpts on pages 4 and 5. Talk with a partner about how the brothers feel about the vineyard at the end of the story.

Cite Text Evidence What evidence helps you understand how the brothers' feelings changed? Write it in the chart.

Clues	How the Brothers Feel

Write I know that the brothers' attitudes changed because the author _____

_____

_____

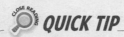

QUICK TIP

When I reread, I can use what characters say to help me understand how they change.

? How do Robert Louis Stevenson and the authors of *The Princess and the Pizza* and "Tomás and His Sons" use words and phrases to help you understand how imagination helps solve problems?

COLLABORATE

Talk About It A counterpane is another word for a bedspread or quilt. Read the poem. Talk with a partner about how the speaker uses imagination to help solve a problem.

Cite Text Evidence Circle clues in the poem that shows the problem. Underline how the speaker uses imagination to solve it.

Write Robert Louis Stevenson and both authors help me see how

imagination helps solve problems by _____

_____

_____

_____

_____

_____

D. Hurst/Alamy

QUICK TIP

I can use text evidence in the poem to understand the importance of imagination. This will help me compare the poem to the selections I read this week.

The Land of Counterpane

When I was sick and lay a-bed,
I had two pillows at my head,
And all my toys beside me lay,
To keep me happy all the day.

And sometimes sent my ships in fleets
All up and down among the sheets;
Or brought my trees and houses out,
And planted cities all about.

I was the giant great and still
That sits upon the pillow-hill,
And sees before him, dale and plain,
The pleasant land of counterpane.

— Robert Louis Stevenson

Experts, Incorporated

*Literature Anthology:
pages 32–41*

? How does the author use dialogue to make the characters seem like people you might know in real life?

COLLABORATE

Talk About It Reread the dialogue on page 35. Does the author do a good job using realistic dialogue between Rodney and his friends? Turn to your partner and talk about whether you agree or not.

Cite Text Evidence Find examples of realistic dialogue and write them in the chart. Write text evidence and explain if the dialogue is effective.

Dialogue	Is it effective?

Write The characters sound like people I might know because the author _____

_____

_____

CLOSE READING

Tip of the Week

When I **reread**, I think about how the author uses dialogue. I look for text evidence to answer questions.

Petra

How does the author build tension when Rodney tries to think of what to write about?

COLLABORATE

Talk About It Reread the third paragraph on page 37. Turn to a partner and talk about how the author describes what Rodney is thinking.

Cite Text Evidence How does the author help you understand how Rodney feels as he tries to think of an idea? Write clues in the web.

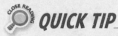
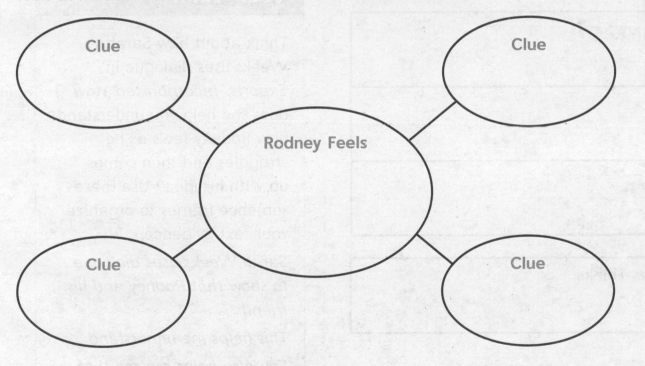

Clue

Clue

Rodney Feels

Clue

Clue

Write The author builds tension by _____

_____

_____

? **How do you know that Rodney is good at defending and describing his idea to others?**

COLLABORATE

Talk About It Reread page 40. Talk with a partner about how Lucas reacts to Rodney's idea.

Cite Text Evidence How does Rodney convince Lucas that his idea is a good one? Write text evidence in the chart below.

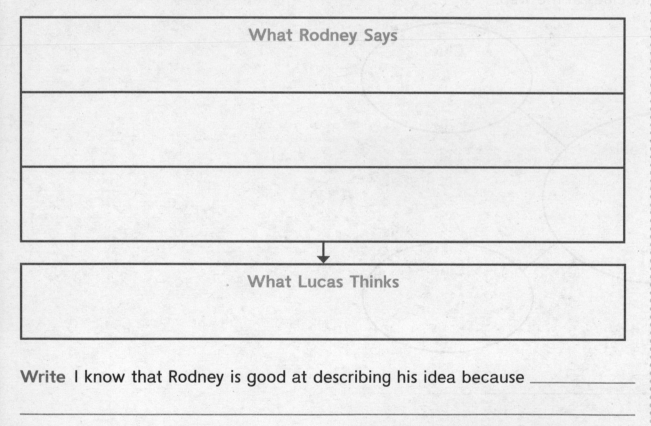

What Rodney Says

↓

What Lucas Thinks

Write I know that Rodney is good at describing his idea because _____

_____

_____

QUICK TIP
I can use dialogue to help me understand how characters feel.

Your Turn

Think about how Sarah Weeks uses dialogue in *Experts, Incorporated.* How does she help you understand how Rodney feels as he struggles and then comes up with his idea? Use these sentence frames to organize your text evidence.

Sarah Weeks uses dialogue to show that Rodney and his friends . . .

This helps me understand . . .

She also helps me see that Rodney can . . .

Go Digital!
Write your response online.

Speaking Out to Stop Bullying

Communities Take a Stand

1. New Hampshire passed a law to stop bullies. The law states that all school staff must be trained to know what bullying looks like. People learn to spot the signs of bullying. The law tells people who see bullying to report it. The state hopes that the law will create bully-free schools.

2. In Midland, Texas, the police take their message to the schools. Police officers make sure to tell students that bullying can be a crime. They want bullies to know that they are accountable for what they do. This means that bullies will be punished if they are caught. The officers tell students who have been bullied or who have seen bullying to report it right away. They make it clear that people have choices. They tell students that anyone can choose to stop being a bully.

Reread and use the prompts to take notes in the text.

"Communities Take a Stand" is a good heading for this section. Reread paragraphs 1 and 2. Underline text evidence that supports this statement.

COLLABORATE

Talk with a partner about what phrase the author repeats. Circle the lines and write them here:

1. _____

2. _____

_____

Young People Speak Out

1   Actress Lauren Potter has a message for lawmakers. She has been speaking out about the bullying of special-needs students. Lauren was born with Down Syndrome. Because she did not look like her classmates, she was teased and called names as a child. She wants laws that will keep people safe from bullies.

Learning to Speak Up

2   It is important for people everywhere to recognize and stand up to all forms of bullying. Everyone has a right to feel safe and to be treated with respect. Likewise, each person has a responsibility to treat others with respect. Report anything that may get in the way of maintaining a safe environment.

In paragraph 1, circle words and phrases that show that Lauren Potter knows what it feels like to be bullied.

How is she making a difference? Underline clues that show you what she is doing.

COLLABORATE

Reread paragraph 2. Talk with a partner about why the author wrote this selection. Mark text evidence in the paragraph that supports your response.

Write one thing the author wants you to learn about bullying here:

_____

_____

? **How do you know how the author feels about bullying?**

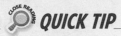

QUICK TIP

When I reread, I analyze the author's words to help me figure out how he feels.

COLLABORATE

Talk About It Look back at the excerpts on pages 11–12. Talk about how the author feels about bullying.

Cite Text Evidence What clues help you understand the author's feelings about bullying? Write text evidence here.

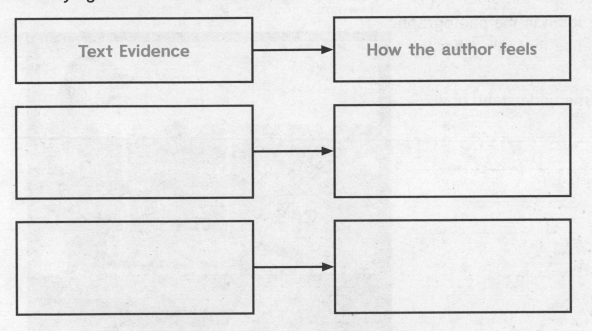

Text Evidence	→	How the author feels
	→	
	→	

Write The author helps me understand how he feels about bullying

by _____

_____

COLLABORATE

? How do the photographer and the authors of *Experts Incorporated* and "Speaking Out to Stop Bullying" help you understand how your actions affect others?

Talk About It Read the caption and look at the photograph. Talk with a partner about what the girls are doing.

Cite Text Evidence What clues help you see how the older girl is affecting the life of the younger girl? Circle them in the photograph. Reread the caption and underline text evidence that tells what the older girl is doing.

Write The photographer and authors help me understand how my actions affect others by _____

_____

_____

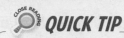
QUICK TIP

I see clues in the photograph that tell me how important it is to treat others in a kind way. This will help me compare it to the texts.

Eric McNatt/Stockbyte/Getty Images

This young baseball player is helping a younger girl learn how to play. They are both part of a program in their community that teams older students with younger ones.

Earthquakes

Literature Anthology:
pages 48–56

? How does the author use photographs to help you understand what it is like to live through an earthquake?

COLLABORATE

Talk About It Reread page 49 and look at the photograph. Talk to a partner about what you see in the photograph.

Cite Text Evidence How does the photograph help you understand what the text says? Write text evidence and tell how it helps.

Text Evidence	Photograph Clues	How It Helps

Write The author uses a photograph to help me understand earthquakes by

_____

_____

CLOSE READING
Tip of the Week

When I **reread**, I can use text features to help me understand information. I look for text evidence to answer questions.

Patrice

Thinkstock Images/Stockbyte/Getty Images

? **How is Dr. Cifuentes' account of the earthquake different from the information in the rest of the selection?**

Talk About It Reread page 51. Turn to a partner and talk about how Dr. Cifuentes describes what it felt like to live through an earthquake.

Cite Text Evidence What words and phrases describe what an earthquake is like? Use this chart to record text evidence.

Dr. Cifuentes' Description	What I Learned

Write Dr. Cifuentes' account helps me understand _____

_____

_____

? How do you know that "Tsunami Terror" is a good heading for this section?

COLLABORATE

Talk About It Reread "Tsunami Terror" on pages 54–55. Turn to a partner and talk about how the author uses words to paint a picture of a tsunami.

Cite Text Evidence What words and phrases show that "Tsunami Terror" is a good heading for this section? Write text evidence in the web.

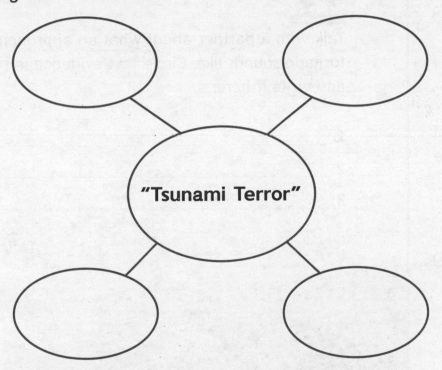

"Tsunami Terror"

Write "Tsunami Terror" is a good heading because _____

_____

_____

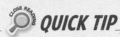

QUICK TIP

When I reread, I can use the author's words and phrases to help me understand about tsunamis.

Your Turn

How does the author use text features to help you understand how earthquakes affect people? Use these sentence frames to organize your text evidence.

The photographs show . . .

The author helps me understand earthquakes better by . . .

I can see that earthquakes . . .

Go Digital!
Write your response online.

Tornado

Raising the Issue

1   When warm and cold air masses collide, the result can be a fast-moving, dangerous force of nature—a tornado. A tornado is a violent windstorm over land. Wind makes a rotating, funnel-shaped cloud that extends toward the ground. As it moves, it picks up debris and objects in its path.

2   Tornadoes are a natural process, especially in flat areas such as the middle of the United States. But tornadoes can also be unpredictable. They may cause destruction on one side of a street yet leave the other side untouched.

3   One way you can tell a tornado is coming is if you spot a funnel cloud. Other warning signs include sounds. An approaching tornado may sound like the rumble of a fast-moving train. It may also sound like a waterfall or like wind whipping into the open windows of a speeding car.

Reread and use the prompts to take notes in the text.

In paragraph 1, underline how the author describes a tornado.

Reread paragraph 3. Make marks in the margin beside the two warning signs that a tornado is approaching.

COLLABORATE

Talk with a partner about what an approaching tornado sounds like. Circle text evidence in paragraph 3 and write it here:

1. _____

2. _____

3. _____

(bkgd) NOAA Photo Library, NOAA Central Library; OAR/ERL/National Severe Storms Laboratory (NSSL)

Tornado Safety

1.   When you hear or see a tornado warning on the Internet, radio, or television, take shelter right away.

2.   If you are in a building with a basement, move to the basement quickly. Get underneath a sturdy, large object, such as a workbench or table.

3.   If you are in a building with no basement, move to the lowest floor. Find a center room away from windows. Crouch down to the floor. Cover your head with your hands.

4.   Avoid being in a car during a tornado. If a tornado is approaching, move inside a building, if possible.

Adam DuBrowa/FEMA

Underline what the author says you should do if you hear a tornado warning. Circle the two safest places in a house during a tornado. Write them here:

1. _____

2. _____

COLLABORATE

Talk with a partner about why the author chose to use the photograph. Underline new information you learned from the caption.

After a tornado hits, it is rated on a scale from 1 to 5. The scale rates the tornado on its wind speed and the damage it has done.

? **What is the author's purpose for including the section "Tornado Safety"?**

Talk About It Reread the excerpt on page 19. Talk with a partner about why the section "Tornado Safety" is important.

Cite Text Evidence What information does the author want you to know about staying safe during a tornado? Write text evidence here.

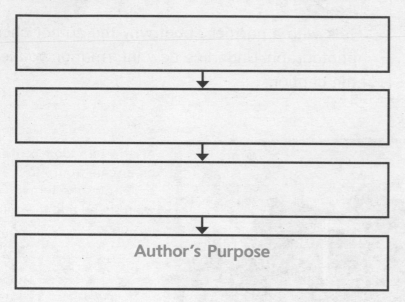

Author's Purpose

Write The author includes tornado safety tips because _____

_____

_____

CLOSE READING
QUICK TIP

When I reread, I can use what the author says to figure out his purpose.

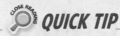

QUICK TIP

I can use clues in the photograph and the selections I read this week to help me compare how natural disasters affect people.

? How does the photographer show the role of the rescue worker after a natural disaster and how does it compare to what you read in *Earthquakes* and "Tornado"?

COLLABORATE

Talk About It Read the caption and look at the photograph. Talk with a partner about how you know how the Coast Guard officer feels about the devastation he sees from Hurricane Katrina.

Cite Text Evidence Circle clues in the photograph that show the effects on both the victims of the hurricane and the rescue worker. Then reread the caption and underline how science and technology help people during natural disasters.

Write The photographer and authors help me understand the role of rescue workers after a natural

disaster by _____

_____

_____

_____

U.S. Coast Guard photograph by Petty Officer 2nd Class NyxoLyno Cangemi

A Coast Guard officer rides in a Jayhawk helicopter over New Orleans on August 30, 2005 after Hurricane Katrina. Many rescue teams searched the city to help people trapped on rooftops following the devastating hurricane.

A Crash Course in Forces and Motion with Max Axiom

Literature Anthology: pages 62–77

? How does the author present information about forces and motion?

COLLABORATE

Talk About It Reread page 64. Talk about why an amusement park is a great setting for this selection.

Cite Text Evidence What words and phrases help you understand forces and motion? Write text evidence and how it helps.

Text Evidence	How It Helps

CLOSE READING

Tip of the Week

When I **reread**, I can use words and phrases to help me understand the text. I look for text evidence to answer questions.

Henry

Write The author presents information about forces and motion by _____

_____

_____

? How does the author use what the characters say and do on the roller coaster to help you understand gravity and inertia?

COLLABORATE

Talk About It Reread pages 68–69. Talk about how a roller coaster works and how the characters are feeling.

Cite Text Evidence How does the author use dialogue to explain gravity and inertia? Write text evidence in the chart.

The Character Says	This Explains

Write The author uses what the characters do and say to _____

_____

_____

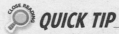
QUICK TIP

I can use these sentence frames when we talk about gravity and inertia.

The author tells me that the characters are . . .

This helps me understand. . .

? **How do the illustrations help you understand mass and gravitational pull?**

COLLABORATE

Talk About It Reread pages 72–73. Use the illustrations to talk about how juggling bowling balls is different than juggling tennis balls.

Cite Text Evidence How does the author show the differences between juggling bowling balls and tennis balls? Compare and contrast below.

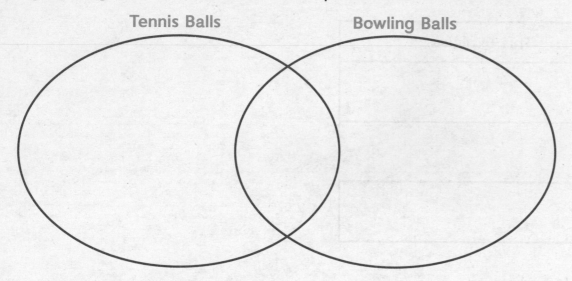

Tennis Balls   Bowling Balls

Write The illustrations help me understand mass and gravitational pull by _____

_____

_____

_____

Your Turn

Think about how authors explain complex ideas. Why does Emily Sohn use real-life examples to show how physical forces work together? Use these sentence frames to organize your text evidence.

Emily Sohn uses real-life examples . . .

This helps me understand . . .

This makes complex ideas about force and motion easier to understand because . . .

Go Digital!
Write your response online.

The Box-Zip Project

1.   "Good morning," Shine said, slipping into his lab coat. "Today's the day! I feel it in my battery!"

2.   Dr. Tank smiled and said, "Now, Shine, we don't feel. We are robots, remember?"

3.   Shine's robot laughter clattered like marbles inside a can. "You got me, Dr. Tank! But, honestly, I think we'll figure out the problem with the silly machine today."

4.   The silly machine, known as the Box-Zip, stood in the middle of the science laboratory looking like a ticket booth.

5.   "Let's hope so, Shine. This project will be history if we're not successful pronto!"

6.   For months, the robots had been attempting to travel in the Box-Zip to Earth. A voyage to planet X to was no problem, and it was twice the distance. They could land on Grolon in a heartbeat. When they traveled to Vinzine, they returned ten minutes before they even left!

Reread and use the prompts to take notes in the text.

Reread paragraphs 1 and 2. How do you know that Shine and Dr. Tank are robots? Underline the clues.

Circle an example of figurative language in paragraph 3. What is the author comparing Shine's laughter to?

_____

Reread paragraph 6. Draw boxes around Shine and Dr. Tank's three successful voyages. Talk with a partner about why the author wants you to know this.

1   "Klugger is no problem, yet we can't manage an Earth landing!" the frustrated Dr. Tank said. "It's ridiculous!"

2   "Come on," Shine encouraged. "Giving up is not an option."

3   Dr. Tank couldn't help but smile at his unfailingly cheerful assistant. Now he regretted not letting Shine get a purple frozen beverage on Klugger.

4   You're absolutely right," said Dr. Tank. "Let's try Earth again."

5   Buckled safely in Box-Zip, Shine began to accelerate to warp times seven blinkers, then twelve blinkers. The world was a distorted blur of colorful motion. The robots' chrome teeth chattered as they whizzed through the galaxies, finally landing with a thud. They peered out the window.

Reread paragraphs 1–3. Circle a clue that tells you something about Shine's character. Then underline the phrase that tells how Dr. Tank feels about Shine.

Write it here.

_____

_____

_____

COLLABORATE

Reread paragraph 5. Talk with a partner about Shine and Dr. Tank's flight to Earth. Make marks in the margin beside words and phrases that help you visualize what is happening.

? **How does the author use dialogue to show how Dr. Tank and Shine feel about solving their problem?**

COLLABORATE

Talk About It Reread the excerpt on page 25. Talk with a partner about how the author gives you a clue that the robots will find a solution to their problem.

Cite Text Evidence How does what the characters say lead to a solution? Use the chart below to record text evidence.

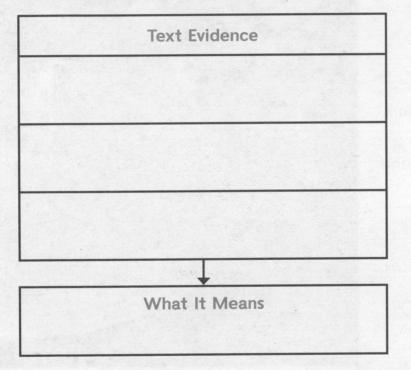

Text Evidence

↓

What It Means

Write Dialogue helps me see how Tank and Dr. Shine feel because _____

_____

 **QUICK TIP**

When I reread, I can use dialogue to understand how characters work together.

? How do NASA's photograph and the authors of *A Crash Course in Forces and Motion with Max Axiom* and "The Box-Zip Project" help you understand how learning about gravity can affect your life?

COLLABORATE

Talk About It Read the caption and look at the photograph. Talk with a partner about what the astronaut is doing and how gravity affects him.

Cite Text Evidence What clues in the photograph and caption show that gravity is important to what the astronaut is doing? Circle evidence in the photograph. Underline text evidence in the caption. Think about how Max Axiom explains gravity and why gravity helps Dr. Tank and Shine solve their problem.

Write The photographer and authors help me understand

_____

_____

_____

_____

**QUICK TIP**

I can use clues in the photograph to help me compare how the authors explain gravity and its effects in this week's selections.

NASA

In this National Aeronautics and Space Administration, or NASA, photograph, Astronaut Mark C. Lee tests equipment in space on September 16, 1994. He is floating about 150 miles above Earth.

Kids in Business

? How does the author help you understand how he feels about young entrepreneurs?

Literature Anthology:
pages 84–87

Talk About It Reread page 85. Turn to a partner and talk about Hayleigh and Joshua's businesses.

Cite Text Evidence What phrases show how the author feels about what Hayleigh and Joshua are doing? Write text evidence in the chart.

Text Evidence	How the Author Feels

Write The author helps me see how he feels about young entrepeneurs by ___

_____

_____

_____

Tip of the Week

When I **reread**, I can use what the author says to understand how he feels.

Kendall

Stockbyte/Getty Images

? Why does the author use a graph to help you see how small change adds up?

COLLABORATE

Talk About It Reread "Kids Count." Turn to your partner and talk about what you learned by looking at the graph.

Cite Text Evidence How does the graph help you understand how small change adds up? Write text evidence.

How Penny Harvest Works	What the Chart Shows	What the Chart Means

Write The author uses a graph to help me _____

_____

QUICK TIP

I can use these sentence frames when we talk about the graph.

The author uses the graph to . . .

This helps me understand . . .

Your Turn

How does the author make his point of view clear in this selection? Cite evidence from the text using these sentence frames.

In each section, the author . . .

This tells me that . . .

Go Digital!
Write your response online.

Starting a Successful Business

1   Becoming an entrepreneur is hard work. But if you're dedicated and have excellent organizational skills, it can be rewarding—sometimes, a small idea can become a very successful business! Neale S. Godfrey, author of *Ultimate Kids' Money Book*, shares these tips for a booming business.

2   Step 1 **Have an innovative idea.**

Suppose you like dogs, have free time, and feel compassionate towards people with busy schedules. Why not start a dog-walking service?

Reread and use the prompts to take notes in the text.

Underline words and phrases in paragraph 1 that tell what the author thinks about what it takes to become an entrepreneur. Write them here.

1. _____

2. _____

3. _____

COLLABORATE

Reread paragraph 2. Talk with a partner about how the author helps you understand what the word *innovative* means.

Circle clues in the illustration that support the text.

How do the illustrations help you understand the steps to starting a business?

Talk About It Reread the excerpt on page 31. Talk with a partner about the illustration and what it shows.

Cite Text Evidence What extra information do you get from the picture? Write clues in the chart.

Text Evidence	Picture Clues

Write The illustration helps me learn more about starting a business by _____

_____

QUICK TIP

When I reread, I can use illustrations to help me understand text.

Integrate

? What message do the authors of "Miller Boy," "Kids in Business," and "Starting a Successful Business" want you to know about running a business?

Talk About It With a partner, read the traditional folk song "Miller Boy." A miller was someone who ground flour into grain and sold it. Talk with a partner about how the song tells what the miller boy does to earn money.

Cite Text Evidence Circle clues in the song that help you understand how the miller boy runs his business.

Write The author of the song and this week's selections want you to know that _____

_____

_____

_____

_____

QUICK TIP

I can use words and phrases in the song to help me understand the songwriter's message. This will help me compare the song to the selections I read this week.

Miller Boy

Oh happy is the miller boy who lives
by the mill,
He takes his toll with a free goodwill;
One hand in the hopper and the other
in the sack,
The ladies step forward and the gents
step back.

Oh happy is the miller boy who lives
by himself,
As the wheel goes 'round,
He gathers in his wealth;
One hand in the hopper and the other
in the sack,
As the wheel goes around the boys
fall back.

The Secret Message

? How does the author help you understand that the parrot and the merchant want different things?

COLLABORATE

Talk About It Reread page 93. Turn to your partner and talk about what the parrot wants and what the merchant wants and how they are different.

Cite Text Evidence What clues help you see that the parrot and merchant want different things? Write text evidence in the chart.

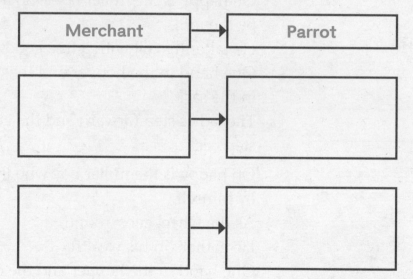

Merchant	→	Parrot
	→	
	→	

Write I know the characters want different things because the author _____

_____

_____

Literature Anthology: pages 90–103

Tip of the Week

When I **reread**, I can think about how the characters are different. I look for text evidence to answer questions.

Marc

Inti St Clair/Blend Images/Getty Images

? **How does the author use dialogue to show you how the merchant really feels about the parrot's life?**

Talk About It Reread the first paragraph on page 97. Turn to your partner and talk about what the merchant tells the parrots in India.

Cite Text Evidence What words and phrases does the merchant use to describe his parrot's life? Write text evidence in the chart.

What the Merchant Says	What the Merchant Thinks

Write The author uses dialogue to help me see that the merchant thinks _____

_____

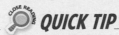

QUICK TIP

I can use these sentence frames when we talk about what the merchant tells the parrots.

The merchant tells the parrots . . .

The author wants me to know that . . .

? How does the illustration help you understand how the parrot's life and the merchant's life will change?

COLLABORATE

Talk About It Reread page 102. Look at the illustration and describe to a partner what the merchant and the parrot are doing.

Cite Text Evidence What clues in the text and the illustration show how the parrot and the merchant's lives will be different? Write text evidence here.

What I Read	What I See	Inferences

Write I know the parrot's life and the merchant's life will change because ____

_____

_____

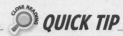
QUICK TIP
As I reread, I can use illustrations to help me understand the characters.

Your Turn

Think about how the author structures the events in this folktale. How does the secret message change things for both the parrot and the merchant? Use these sentence frames to organize your text evidence.

The author begins the folktale by describing . . .

She uses cause and effect to show . . .

This helps me figure out that the parrot . . .

Go Digital!
Write your response online.

The Fox and the Goat

1   Francis Fox had already gobbled one mouse, but one was never enough to fill his stomach. His greed got him into trouble as he chased the second mouse. He did not see the old well and tumbled nose over tail down into the cold water. Looking up, Francis saw a circle of blue sky and jumped as high as possible—but he could not reach the top.

2   "How will I get out?" howled Francis.

3   Just then, the sound of chewing echoed down in the well, and Francis saw Gordo Goat at the edge of the well's opening. Francis knew that Gordo would do anything for food and water. He made loud slurping noises to attract the old goat's attention.

4   "This water is delicious," the sly fox shouted. "Don't you want a thirst-quenching drink?"

5   Gordo had been chewing on thorns and weeds, and he definitely needed water to wash down his food. "Sure," he said, "but how will I get out?"

6   "We'll help each other," said Francis with a smile that showed all of his teeth.

Reread and use the prompts to take notes in the text.

Reread paragraphs 1–3. Underline the sentence that tells what Francis Fox is like.

Circle clues that help you know what Gordo Goat is like.

COLLABORATE

Reread paragraphs 4–6. Talk with a partner about how the dialogue between Francis and Gordo hint at events to come. Make a mark beside the sentences that show that Francis has a plan. Write them here:

_____

_____

_____

_____

7   Gordo was not sure whether Francis was being honest, but the goat was very thirsty. He jumped into the well, and when his thirst was quenched he looked up.

8   "Now . . .how do we get out of here?" he asked.

9   "Easy," said Francis. "Put your front hooves on the wall, and I'll climb on your back and jump out of the well. Then I'll go get help for you," said Francis, grinning. "Honest."

10   "Okay. But hurry back," said Gordo, placing his hooves against the stones.

11   In a flash, Francis leaped onto Gordo's back and then climbed onto the goat's horns to spring out of the well. Francis looked back down at the goat and waved. "Didn't anyone ever tell you to look before you leap?" The fox chuckled as he ran off, leaving Gordo to find his own way out of the well.

Reread paragraphs 7–9. Underline three phrases that show that Francis is not being honest. Write them here:

1. _____

2 _____

3. _____

COLLABORATE

Reread the rest of the excerpt. Talk with a partner about what Francis does to Gordo. How do you know that Francis is not sorry? Circle the text evidence to support your discussion.

? How does the author use what the characters say and do at the beginning of the fable to help you figure out how the story will end?

COLLABORATE

Talk About It Reread the excerpts on pages 37–38. With a partner, talk about how the author reveals what kind of characters Francis and Gordo are.

Cite Text Evidence What clues does the author give you about Francis's character? Write the clues in the web.

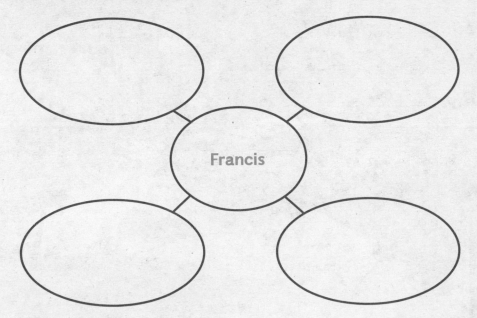

Francis

Write The author helps me figure out what will happen in the fable by _____

_____

_____

_____

CLOSE READING

QUICK TIP

When I reread, I can use descriptions and dialogue to help me understand what characters do.

? How do the artist and the authors of *The Secret Message* and "The Fox and the Goat" show how animal stories can teach lessons?

COLLABORATE

Talk About It Look at the illustration and read the caption. Talk with a partner about what the illustration shows about the mouse's character.

Cite Text Evidence Circle clues in the illustration that show what the mouse is like. Then underline text evidence in the caption that supports your discussion about the mouse's character. In the space below the illustration, write the lesson you learn from the mouse.

Write The authors and artist help me see how

animal tales can teach lessons by _____

_____

_____

_____

Ivy Close Images/Alamy

QUICK TIP

I see a tiny mouse trying to free a large lion. This will help me compare the messages in text and art.

In this illustration from Aesop's fable, "The Lion and the Mouse," the tiny mouse helps free the mighty lion from a hunter's trap.

Ranita, The Frog Princess

Literature Anthology,
pages 108–123

? How does the author use what the characters say to help you understand what the Spanish words mean?

COLLABORATE

Talk About It Reread the dialogue on page 112. Turn to your partner and talk about what helps you to understand the Spanish words in italics.

Cite Text Evidence What clues help you figure out each word's meaning? Record the words and clues here.

Words	Text Evidence

Write I know what the Spanish words mean because the author _____

_____

CLOSE READING **Tip** of the **Week**

When I **reread**, I can use dialogue to help me figure out words I don't know. I look for text evidence to answer questions.

Tori

mamahoohooba/Alamy

? **How do you know how the other characters feel about Felipe?**

COLLABORATE

Talk About It Reread page 114. Turn to your partner and talk about how the author shows what the other characters in the play are feeling.

Cite Text Evidence What words describe how the characters feel about Felipe? Use text evidence to explain how you know.

Character		Text Evidence
	→	
	→	
	→	
	→	

Write I know how the other characters feel about Felipe because the author

_____

_____

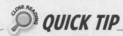
QUICK TIP

I can use these sentence frames when we talk about what the other characters think.

The author shows how the characters feel by . . .

This helps me understand that . . .

? **How does the author help you understand the relationship between Felipe and Pepe?**

COLLABORATE

Talk About It Reread page 119. Turn to your partner and talk about what Felipe and Pepe say and do.

Cite Text Evidence What clues show you how Felipe and Pepe feel about each other? Write text evidence and explain how it helps you know.

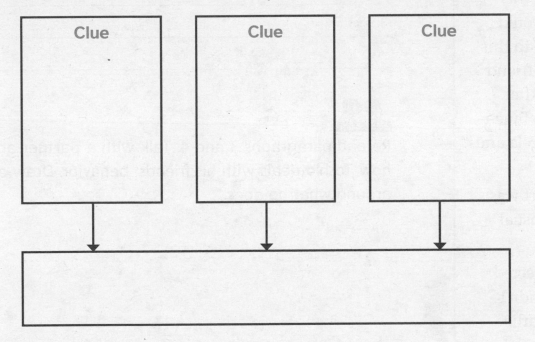

Clue	Clue	Clue

Write The author helps me understand Felipe and Pepe by _____
_____
_____

QUICK TIP

When I reread, I can think about the way the author describes what the characters say and do.

Your Turn

How does the author use descriptive language and stage directions to help you understand how the characters in the play change? Use these sentence frames to organize your text evidence.

Carmen Agra Deedy uses stage directions to . . .

She describes how each character feels by . . .

This helps me understand how they change because . . .

Go Digital!
Write your response online.

The Moonlight Concert Mystery

1   The last rays of sunlight slipped down through the sea as Toshio the Turtle, world-famous detective, sighed with relief. The workday was finally over, and the Moonlight Concert would soon begin. He had been looking forward to this night for months, although he wished his friend Jack the Jellyfish could have joined him. After the concert, Toshio was off to Florida for a much-needed break. As he was packing up, Angela and Charlie rushed into his office.

2   "Can you believe the Moonlight Concert was canceled?" Charlie the Crab asked in his usual cranky manner.

3   "Now, now," Angela the Angelfish corrected. "Where are your manners, Charlie? You didn't even say hello!" She smiled sweetly as Charlie rolled his eyes.

4   Toshio was used to this behavior from the pair, so he turned to Angela and asked, "What's all this about the concert being canceled?"

Reread and use the prompts to take notes in the text.

Underline clues in paragraph 1 that tell how Toshio the Turtle feels about the concert.

Circle how he feels about Jack the Jellyfish. Write text evidence here:

_____

_____

_____

COLLABORATE

Reread paragraphs 3 and 4. Talk with a partner about how Toshio deals with his friends' behavior. Draw a box around what he does.

1. Toshio paused to pick up a crumpled sheet of paper before following the others into the cave. As he pulled back the seaweed curtain, Toshio heard the coral hit the drums in a familiar rhythm. Suddenly the lights came up, and everyone shouted, "Surprise, Toshio!"

2. Toshio couldn't help but smile. "My friends, you have outdone yourselves in creating this great mystery. I never guessed that you were planning a going-away party for me! What a delightful surprise!"

3. As the music swelled inside Mermaid Cave, Toshio read the crumpled note. *Have everyone gather in Mermaid Cave for tonight's surprise! Don't forget my drumsticks! –Jamming Jack Jellyfish.* Toshio chuckled to himself and tucked the page into his notebook. He couldn't think of a better way to spend his last night before setting out on his next big adventure.

Reread paragraph 1. Circle two clues that help add suspense to the mystery. Write them here:

1. _____

_____

2. _____

_____

COLLABORATE

With a partner reread the rest of the excerpt. Underline how the author indicates what Toshio reads in the crumpled note. Talk about how you know who wrote it.

Make a mark in the margin beside the author of the note.

? **How does the author use what Jack the Jellyfish does to create suspense?**

Talk About It Reread both excerpts on pages 44–45. Talk with a partner about the clues about Jack the Jellyfish at the beginning and end of the mystery.

Cite Text Evidence What clues does the author use to help build suspense? Write text evidence here and explain how it builds suspense.

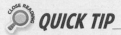 **QUICK TIP**

When I reread, I can use clues in the beginning of a mystery to help me understand what happens at the end.

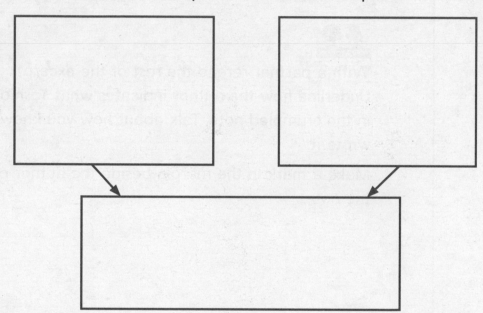

Write The author uses Jack the Jellyfish to create suspense by _____

_____

_____

? How does Mary Howitt use words and phrases to help me visualize the characters in her poem and how is it similar to the way the authors describe the characters in *Ranita, The Frog Princess* and "The Moonlight Concert Mystery"?

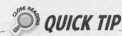

QUICK TIP

I can use the poet's words and phrases to visualize the characters. This will help me compare it to the selections I read this week.

COLLABORATE

Talk About It Read the excerpt from *The Spider and the Fly*. Talk with a partner about how the spider tricks and then traps the fly.

Cite Text Evidence Circle words and phrases in the poem that make the spider seem human. Underline text evidence that makes the fly seem human.

Write Mary Howitt uses words and phrases to help me visualize

_____

_____

_____

_____

from The Spider and the Fly

Alas, alas! how very soon this silly little Fly,

Hearing his wily, flattering words,
came slowly flitting by;

With buzzing wings she hung aloft,
then near and nearer drew, -

Thinking only of her brilliant eyes,
and green and purple hue;

Thinking only of her crested head
- poor foolish thing! At last,

Up jumped the cunning Spider,
and fiercely held her fast.

He dragged her up his winding stair,
into his dismal den.

—by Mary Howitt

The Buffalo Are Back

? Why does the author want you to picture a healthy and thriving prairie at the beginning of the selection?

COLLABORATE

Talk About It Reread the first paragraph on page 131. Turn to your partner and describe the setting of this selection.

Cite Text Evidence Explain how the author uses words and phrases to paint a picture of life on the prairie. Cite and explain text evidence.

Sensory Language	What I Visualize

Write The author wants me to visualize what the prairie looks like because

_____

_____

Literature Anthology:
pages 130–145

CLOSE READING

Tip of the Week

When I **reread**, I can think about how the author uses words and phrases. I look for text evidence to answer questions.

Zoe

Comstock Images/Stockbyte/Getty Images

? Why does the author compare and contrast the different groups of people on the prairie?

COLLABORATE

Talk About It Reread the first three paragraphs on page 135. Talk with a partner about how the people on the prairie were alike and different.

Cite Text Evidence Which groups of people did the most damage to the buffalo, the Indians, and the prairie? Write text evidence in the chart.

Groups of people	Text Evidence

Write The author compares and contrasts the different groups of people to

_____

_____

QUICK TIP

I can use these sentence frames when we talk about how the different groups are alike and different.

The fur hunters and the explorers . . .

But the settlers and the soldiers . . .

? **Why is the author's description of the secluded meadow an important part of the selection?**

COLLABORATE

Talk About It With a partner, reread the second paragraph on page 140. Talk about how the author describes the secluded meadow.

Cite Text Evidence If you were flying over the secluded meadow in a plane, what would you see? Use the author's description to visualize and draw a map.

Write The author's description of the meadow is important because _____

_____

_____

QUICK TIP
CLOSE READING

I can visualize what the author wrote about the secluded meadow. It will help me create my map.

Your Turn

Think about how the author uses repetition. Why does she begin and end the selection with the birth of an orange buffalo calf? Use these sentence frames to organize your text evidence.

Jean Craighead George states ". . ."

Her point is that . . .

This is important because . . .

Go Digital!
Write your response online.

Energy in the Ecosystem

Forest Food Chain

[1] The forest food chain begins with organisms that make their own food. They are called *producers*. Grasses, trees, and other green plants are producers that feed forest animals. Organisms that cannot make their own food are known as *consumers*. Any animal that eats plants or plant products is a consumer. Some forest consumers, such as rabbits, are herbivores that eat only plants. Other mammals, such as voles and mice, are *omnivores*. They eat plants as well insects, worms, and grubs.

[2] Higher up on the food chain are organisms that eat other consumers. In the forest, birds of prey such as owls, occupy this link in the chain. Owls are *carnivores*, which means they eat only other animals. Since owls cannot make their own food, they are also consumers in the food chain.

Reread and use the prompts to take notes in the text.

Underline two examples in paragraph 1 showing how the author helps you understand what the words in italics mean. Write those two ways here:

1. _____

2. _____

  _____

COLLABORATE

Talk with a partner about how the author uses both text and the diagram to explain the forest food chain. Add more examples from the text to the diagram.

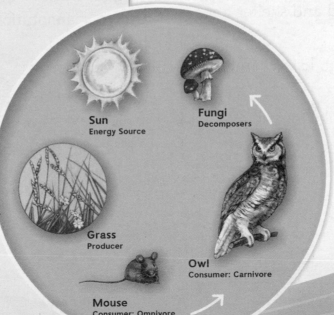

Sun
Energy Source

Fungi
Decomposers

Grass
Producer

Owl
Consumer: Carnivore

Mouse
Consumer: Omnivore

Back to the Cycle

3   Fungi play a different role in the food chain. They are decomposers. Decomposers recycle all the wastes and remains from plants and animals back into the ecosystem. The dead material becomes soil nutrients, which help plants grow. With sunlight and water, the cycle begins again.

4   When an owl eats a mouse or a vole, it digests the meat and organs of those animals. However, owls cannot digest fur, teeth, or bones. These are formed into oval pellets. The owl throws up these balls of fur and bone after every meal. Owl pellets are often found on the ground and around owl nesting places. They provide food and shelter for the moths, beetles and fungi.

5   If you are near a forest at night, listen carefully. Do you hear it?

6   "Who cooks for you? Who cooks for you all?"

Reread paragraph 3. Circle the words the author uses to help you understand how the food chain is like a cycle. Write them here:

_____

_____

_____

COLLABORATE

Reread paragraph 4. Talk about the steps in the forest food chain. Number the steps from 1 to 4 in the margin near each clue.

Why is "Back to the Cycle" a good title for this section? Use your annotations to support your response. Write it here:

_____

_____

_____

? **How does the author use repetition to organize the information in this selection?**

 **QUICK TIP**
When I reread, I analyze how the author uses repetition.

> One call can be heard often from the forest. It sounds like, "Who cooks for you? Who cooks for you all?"
>
> HOO HOO Hoo-hoo! HOO HOO Hoo awwww!

COLLABORATE

Talk About It Reread this excerpt from the selection. Then reread paragraphs 5 and 6 on page 52. With a partner, compare the texts.

Cite Text Evidence In the excerpt above, underline the sentence the author repeats. Find a clue that explains what both sentences mean. Circle it.

Write The author uses repetition to _____

_____

_____

? How is the way the artist uses layers in his painting similar to the way the authors organize text in *The Buffalo Are Back* or "Energy in the Ecosystem"?

COLLABORATE

Talk About It With a partner, discuss what you see in Paul Gauguin's painting. Choose some of the images in the painting and talk about how they depend on each other to live.

Cite Text Evidence Look at the painting. There is a layer of animals across the bottom. Draw a line to separate that layer from the layer above it. Work with your partner to find four different layers and mark them. Then circle three living things that depend on each other to live.

Write Paul Gauguin's use of layers is similar to _____

_____

_____

_____

_____

_____

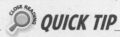
QUICK TIP
I see layers of living things in the painting. This will help me compare text to art.

Courtesy National Gallery of Art, Washington

French painter Paul Gauguin painted "Haystacks in Brittany" in 1890. It is an oil painting on canvas.

Spiders

Literature Anthology, pages 152-167

? How do the author's words and phrases help you visualize how a spider eats its prey?

COLLABORATE

Talk About It Reread page 156. Turn to your partner and talk about the descriptive words the author uses to describe how the spider eats.

Cite Text Evidence What image does the author create with these descriptive words? Cite text evidence from the paragraph.

Words	What I Visualize

Write The author helps me visualize how a spider eats its prey by _____

_____

_____

CLOSE READING **Tip of the Week**

When I **reread**, I can use the author's words to help me visualize. I look for text evidence to answer questions.

Grant

Nathan Blaney/Stockbyte/Getty Images

How do you know how the author feels about the spider's senses?

COLLABORATE

Talk About It Reread page 160. Turn to your partner and talk about the way the author describes what the spider can do.

Cite Text Evidence What words and phrases help you understand how the author feels about the spider's senses? Write text evidence and explain.

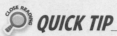
QUICK TIP

I can use these sentence frames when we talk about the author's point of view.

The author uses words that . . .

This helps me understand that he feels . . .

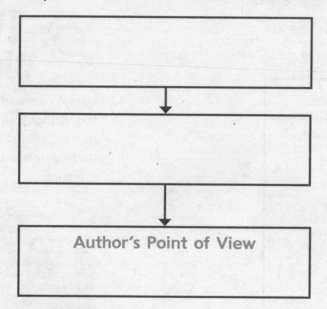

Author's Point of View

Write I know how the author feels about the spider's senses because _____

_____

_____

? How do the text features help you understand more about orb web spiders?

COLLABORATE

Talk About It Reread page 167. Look at the photograph and read the caption. Turn to your partner and talk about what new information you learned.

Cite Text Evidence What details in the text features give you more information about orb spiders? Write text evidence in the chart.

Text Evidence	Photograph	Caption

Write The author uses text features to _____

_____

Your Turn

Think about how Nic Bishop uses text features to tell about spiders. How do they help you understand his point of view about spiders? Use these sentence frames to organize your text evidence.

Nic Bishop uses text features to . . .

He shows that spiders are . . .

That helps me understand that he thinks spiders . . .

Go Digital!
Write your response online.

Anansi and the Birds

1. Anansi always welcomed a challenge. His attempts to fool merchants out of their riches and lions from their jungle thrones made for exciting adventures. Today he would show those haughty birds that he could fly with the best of them.

2. He begged a feather from every bird he could find to create his own pair of wings, and then he began to practice flying. Anansi's wings camouflaged him well, and he looked just like a bird.

3. "Hoot!" the old owl chided under the moon. "A spider is not meant for the sky. Why do you try to be something you are not?"

4. "Mind your business, owl," Anansi replied angrily. "You are a predator, so go hunt some mice!"

5. Anansi followed the birds to their feast on top of a mountain peak. He helped himself to their fare, shoving birds aside to get his fill. When he was full, he fell into a deep sleep.

Reread and use the prompts to take notes in the text.

Circle text evidence in paragraphs 1 and 2 that tells you about Anansi's character.

COLLABORATE

Reread paragraphs 3 and 4. Talk with a partner about the relationship between Anansi and the old owl. Underline the dialogue that helps you understand how they feel about each other.

Then reread paragraph 5. How does the author hint that something unpleasant might happen to Anansi? Draw a box around the clue. Write it here:

_____

_____

6   Angrily, the birds took back the feathers from his wings and then left, all except for one crow. When Anansi awoke, he realized what had happened and begged the crow to help him get down the mountain.

7   "Of course," the crow replied slyly as he shoved Anansi over a cliff.

8   "Aaaayeeee!" shouted Anansi. Unable to fly, he tumbled helplessly through the air.

9   The old owl appeared before him, asking, "Why didn't you listen, Anansi? You are not a bird!"

10   "Please help me, owl!" pleaded Anansi.

11   The owl urged Anansi, "Push in your belly!" When he did, threads of silk shot out behind him. The owl caught them and tied them to a high branch. Dangling by threads, Anansi realized the owl was right. From that day on, he stuck to spinning webs instead of trying to be something he was not.

Read paragraphs 6–9. Circle the words and phrases that describe how the birds feel about Anansi and what they did.

COLLABORATE

With a partner, read paragraphs 10 and 11. Talk about how the owl helps Anansi. Number the steps in the margin.

Then underline the sentence that tells how the spider feels about the owl now. Write text evidence here:

_____

_____

? How does the author help you visualize the characters' traits to help you understand the lesson Anansi learns?

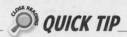 **QUICK TIP**
When I reread, I can use how the author describes each character to help me understand what they do.

COLLABORATE

Talk About It Reread the excerpt on page 58. Talk about each character and how it helps you understand what they do.

Cite Text Evidence What words and phrases help you identify each character's traits? Record text evidence.

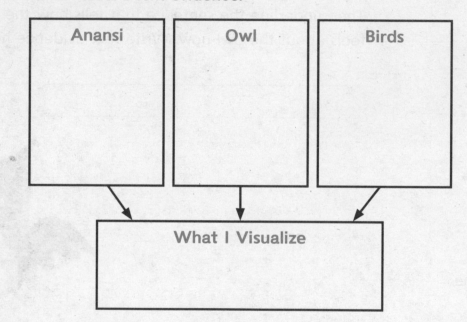

Anansi	Owl	Birds

What I Visualize

Write The author helps me visualize the characters' traits to help me _____

_____

_____

_____

? **How does the photographer use the background in his photograph to show how seahorses are unique and how is that similar to the authors' use of text features and descriptions in *Spider* and "Anansi and the Birds"?**

Kris Wiktor/Alamy

Talk About It Use the photograph and caption to talk about the seahorse. Discuss how the photograph shows how it survives.

Cite Text Evidence With a pencil, trace around the outside of the leafy dragon seahorse in the photograph. Circle clues that show how the seahorse survives. Reread the caption and underline what the animal does to protect itself from its enemies.

Write The photographer and authors show how animals are

unique by _____

_____

_____

QUICK TIP

I can use clues in the photograph to compare how the other animals I read about this week are unique.

The leafy dragon seahorse, or leafy seadragon, lives in the waters off the southern coast of Australia. They swim among the boulders and sea grasses around the reefs. These animals rely on their looks to keep them safe.

Poetry

? How does the author use figurative language to help you visualize bats?

Literature Anthology, pages 172-174

COLLABORATE

Talk About It Reread page 173. Talk with a partner about what bats look like during the day and what they look like at dusk.

Cite Text Evidence What words and phrases help you picture the bats during the day and at night? Write text evidence in the chart.

Text Evidence	What I Visualize

Write The author helps me visualize bats by _____

_____

_____

CLOSE READING

Tip of the Week

When I **reread**, I can think about how the poet uses words and phrases. I look for text evidence to answer questions.

Katia

Todd Warnock/Digital Vision/Getty Images

? How does each poet use words and phrases to create a different mood?

COLLABORATE

Talk About It With a partner, reread "The Grasshopper Springs" and "Fireflies at Dusk." Talk about how each poem makes you feel.

Cite Text Evidence What words help to create a certain mood in the poems? Write and explain text evidence.

Poem	Text Evidence	Why is this effective?
"The Grasshopper Springs"		
"Fireflies at Dusk"		

Write Each poet uses words and phrases to create a mood by _____

_____

QUICK TIP

I can use these sentence frames when we talk about the poems.
When I read "The Grasshopper Springs," I feel . . .

When I read "Fireflies at Dusk," I feel . . .

Your Turn

Describe how the poets use their inspiration to convey their point of view about each animal or insect. Use these sentence frames to help organize your text evidence.
In each poem, the poet is inspired by . . .

In "The Sandpiper," the poet describes . . .

In "The Grasshopper Springs" and "Fireflies at Dusk," the poet describes how . . .

Go Digital!
Write your response online.

Fog

? **How does the poet use words and phrases to help you visualize how fog is like a cat?**

Talk About It Reread page 176 aloud to a partner. Talk about how the poet describes what fog is like.

Cite Text Evidence What words and phrases help you picture how fog is like a cat? Write text evidence in the chart.

Text Evidence	What I Visualize

Write The poet helps me visualize how fog is like a cat by _____

_____

_____

QUICK TIP
I can use the poet's words and phrases to help me visualize.

"White Cat Winter"

? **How do the poets use words and phrases to create mood?**

COLLABORATE

Talk About It Reread the poems on pages 176 and 177. Talk with a partner about how each of the poems makes you feel.

Cite Text Evidence What words and phrases help create mood in each of the poems? Write text evidence and tell how it helps.

Text Evidence	Mood

Write The poets create mood by _____

_____

_____

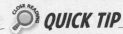

Integrate

? How does Lewis Carroll use the crocodile as inspiration for his poem and how is that similar to the way the poets were inspired by animals in the poems you read this week?

COLLABORATE

Talk About It Read "How Doth the Little Crocodile." Talk with a partner about how Lewis Carroll describes the crocodile.

Cite Text Evidence Circle words and phrases in the poem that help you visualize the crocodile. Draw a box around what Lewis Carroll does that shows he was inspired by the animal.

Write The way Lewis Carroll uses animals for inspiration is like _____

_____

_____

_____

_____

_____

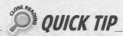
QUICK TIP

I can use the way the poet describes a crocodile to help me see how he is inspired by animals. This will help me compare this poem to the ones I read this week.

How Doth the Little Crocodile

How doth the little crocodile
Improve his shining tail,
And pour the waters of the Nile
On every golden scale!

How cheerfully he seems to grin,
How neatly spreads his claws,
And welcomes little fishes in
With gently smiling jaws!

— Lewis Carroll

Reread

The Cricket in Times Square

Literature Anthology: pages 178–193

? How does the author use Tucker and Chester's first meeting to help you understand the characters?

COLLABORATE

Talk About It Reread the dialogue on page 180. Turn to a partner and discuss what you learned about Tucker and Chester from their conversation.

Cite Text Evidence How does the author use dialogue to show what Tucker and Chester are like? Write your evidence in the chart.

Character	What the Character Says	What This Shows
Tucker		
Chester		

Write The author uses Tucker and Chester's first meeting to _____

_____

Tip of the Week

CLOSE READING

When I **reread**, I can focus on dialogue to help me understand what the characters are like. I look for text evidence to answer questions.

Shaun

Unit 3 • Week 1 • Friendship **67**

How do you know how Chester feels about being in New York City?

COLLABORATE

Talk About It Reread pages 186 and 187. Talk with a partner about how Chester feels about being in New York City.

Cite Text Evidence What clues in the dialogue help you know how Chester is feeling? Fill in the chart with text evidence.

QUICK TIP

I can use these sentence frames when we talk about Chester's feelings.

Chester says . . .

This helps me understand that he feels . . .

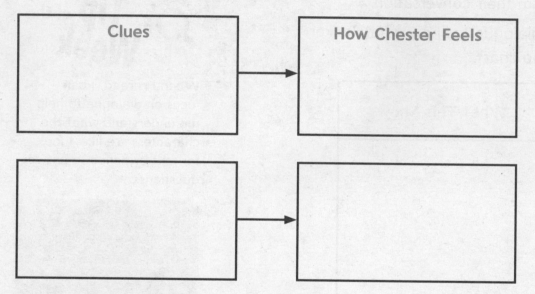

Clues		How Chester Feels
	→	
	→	

Write I know how Chester feels about New York City because the author _____

_____

_____

? **How does the author show how Chester and Tucker are different?**

COLLABORATE

Talk About It Reread paragraphs 3–5 on page 191. Turn to your partner and talk about why Chester is confused.

Cite Text Evidence How does the author show what Chester is confused about? Write why that's important in the chart.

Text Evidence	Why It's Important

Write I know that Chester and Tucker are different because the author _____

_____

_____

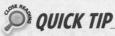

QUICK TIP
CLOSE READING

When I reread, I can use what the author writes about the characters to understand how they are different.

Your Turn

How does George Selden use dialogue to show how Chester and Tucker's friendship develops throughout the story? Use these sentence frames to help organize your text evidence.

George Selden uses Chester and Tucker's first meeting to . . .

He shows how they feel by . . .

This helps me understand that their friendship . . .

Go Digital!
Write your response online.

The Girl and the Chenoo

1   The ferocious Chenoo of the North was a cold-hearted predator and a thief. With one swipe, the Chenoo's talons uprooted beans, corns, and squash to satisfy his enormous hunger. Fish jumped out of the water at the sight of his terrifying figure. Whenever the Chenoo howled, hailstones fell from the sky, battering the homes of my people.

2   So my brothers and I were prepared for war when we followed the Chenoo's giant footprints to our winter home. Instead we found my sister dressing the monster's wounds.

3   My sister never spoke much, but her quiet nature and caring ways were complementary to the skill of my brothers and me as hunters. Without a word, she gathered firewood, tanned hides, repaired the wigwam, and prepared our meals.

4   She turned nervously toward us. "Brothers," she whispered. "Grandfather will be joining us for dinner tonight."

5   Puzzled, my brothers and I looked at each other.

Reread and use the prompts to take notes in the text.

Circle words and phrases in paragraph 1 that describe the Chenoo.

Reread paragraphs 2 and 3. How does the author describe the narrator's sister? Underline clues that help you visualize what she's like.

COLLABORATE

Talk with a partner about what the narrator's sister says in paragraph 4. Draw a box around it. How does the author use this to show how the Chenoo is feared?

Use your annotations to support your response.

_____

_____

_____

1   The Chenoo snorted and disappeared into the woods. He returned with four large moose. My sister prepared a feast unlike any other we had ever eaten.

2   I wondered how long our sister could keep this treacherous beast tame. The Chenoo was not trustworthy. Surely he would soon destroy everything in his path. But somehow my sister's kindness changed his ways.

3   One warm night, my sister turned to the Chenoo and said, "Grandfather, it's time to return to the village."

4   He nodded and walked up to the fire. He had always kept away from the fire, but now he asked for more firewood. My sister added wood until the flames shot up over his head. He coughed and moaned.

5   "Grandfather?" my worried sister called.

6   Once the smoke cleared, the Chenoo had become a wrinkled old man. Hunched over the fire, he coughed up a piece of ice shaped like a Chenoo – it was his icy heart!

Reread paragraphs 1 and 2. Underline a clue that shows what caused the Chenoo to be changed. Write text evidence here:

_____

_____

COLLABORATE

Reread the rest of the excerpt. Talk with a partner about how the narrator's sister felt as the Chenoo stood near the fire. Make a mark next to the text evidence that supports your discussion.

Circle words and phrases that help you visualize what happens to the Chenoo at the end of the legend.

? **How does the author show how the Chenoo changes in the legend?**

 **QUICK TIP**

When I reread, I can use how the author describes what the characters do to help me see how they change.

COLLABORATE

Talk About It Reread the excerpts on pages 70 and 71. With a partner, talk about how the Chenoo changes.

Cite Text Evidence What clues does the author use to help you see how the Chenoo has changed? Write them in the chart.

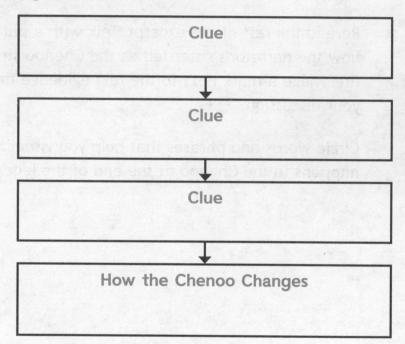

Clue

↓

Clue

↓

Clue

↓

How the Chenoo Changes

Write The author shows how the Chenoo changes by _____

_____

_____

Integrate

? **What does the artist want you to know about the people in his painting and how does it compare with the way the authors help you get to know the characters in *The Cricket in Times Square* and "The Girl and the Chenoo"?**

COLLABORATE

Talk About It Look carefully at the painting. With a partner, discuss what the women in William Merritt Chase's painting are doing.

Cite Text Evidence What clues in the painting help you understand the women's relationship? Circle evidence that shows information about their visit. Then read the caption and underline text evidence that helps you understand more about the painting.

Write William Merritt Chase and the authors of *The Cricket in Times Square* and "The Girl and the Chenoo"

help me understand their characters by _____

_____

QUICK TIP

I can use the title of the painting to help me understand what it shows. Then I can compare it to the characters in the selections I read this week.

This painting is titled "A Friendly Call." It was painted by William Merritt Chase, an American painter, in 1895. It is an oil painting on canvas.

Aguinaldo

Literature Anthology:
pages 198–209

? **How do you know how Marilia feels about going on the field trip?**

COLLABORATE

Talk About It Reread paragraphs 1–4 on page 203. Turn to your partner and talk about Marilia's last thing left to do.

Cite Text Evidence What clues help you understand what Marilia was feeling about going on the field trip? Write evidence and what it means in the chart.

CLOSE READING
Tip of the Week

When I **reread**, I can pay attention to the characters' actions. Then I can find text evidence to help me understand how they feel.

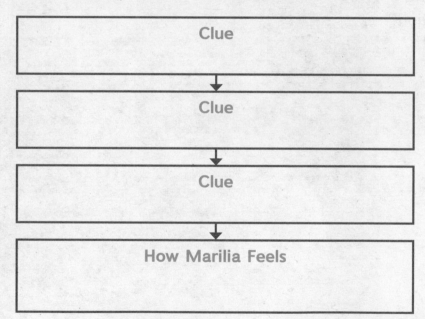

Clue

↓

Clue

↓

Clue

↓

How Marilia Feels

Ava

Write I know how Marilia feels about going on the field trip because the author _____

_____

Christa Paustenbaugh Photography/Moment/Getty Images

? How does the author use dialogue to show the relationship between Elenita and Marilia?

Talk About It Reread the first four paragraphs on page 207. Turn to your partner and discuss what Elenita and Marilia talk about.

Cite Text Evidence What clues help you figure out how they are getting along? Write text evidence in the chart.

Clues	Elenita and Marilia

Write The author uses dialogue to show that Elenita and Marilia are _____

_____

_____

 **QUICK TIP**

I can use these sentence frames when we talk about how Elenita and Marilia are getting along.

The author uses dialogue to show that . . .

This makes Marilia feel . . .

? How does what Marilia tells Margarita on the bus trip back to school help you understand how she feels?

COLLABORATE

Talk About It Reread the last three paragraphs on page 208. Turn to your partner and talk about what Margarita and Marilia talked about on the bus.

Cite Text Evidence What does Marilia say that shows how she feels? Write text evidence in the chart.

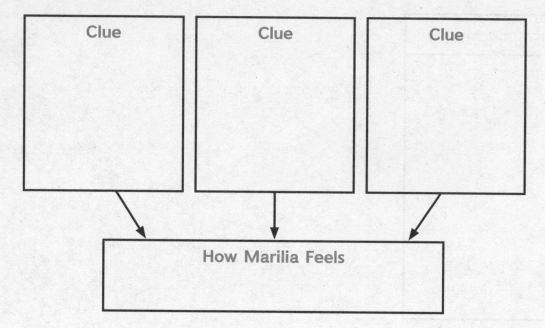

Clue	Clue	Clue

How Marilia Feels

Write The author uses Margarita and Marilia's conversation to help show that

_____

_____

QUICK TIP
When I reread, I can use what the characters say to understand their actions.

Your Turn

How does Marilia change from the beginning of the story to the end? Use these sentence frames to organize your text evidence.

The author shows how Marilia feels at the beginning of the story by . . .

She uses dialogue to show . . .

By the end of the story, I understand that Marilia . . .

Go Digital!
Write your response online.

Partaking in Public Service

There is no doubt about it:

1   Volunteering is an important part of American life. About 27% of us volunteer in some way. This means that one American out of every four is performing a public service. Many volunteers are teens and children. In fact, in the last 20 years, the number of teen volunteers in this country has doubled. Youth service organizations, such as 4-H clubs, have grown in popularity.

2   Kids join local volunteer groups to give back to their communities. They work together to help others and to improve their schools and neighborhoods. Community projects may include planting gardens or collecting food and clothing. Some kids raise money for local charities. The volunteer opportunities are limitless.

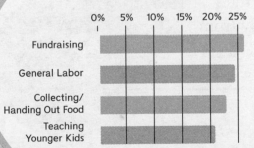

Top Four Volunteer Activities for Kids

Reread and use the prompts to take notes in the text.

Underline the clue in paragraph 1 that tells how the author feels about volunteering. Circle two examples in paragraph 1 that support the author's statement.

COLLABORATE

Reread paragraph 2 and look at the bar graph. Talk with a partner about how the bar graph helps you understand how kids volunteer.

In the bar graph, circle the top volunteer activity for kids. Draw a box around the activity that about 21 percent of kids volunteer to do.

1   Katie Stagliano had a gallant idea that started with a tiny seedling. When Katie was nine years old, she brought home a cabbage seed from school. From that seed, she grew a 40-pound cabbage in her garden. The cabbage was as big as Katie. She donated it to a soup kitchen, and it helped to feed almost 300 people. After that, Katie never looked back. She has donated thousands of pounds of produce to people in need.

2   Evan Green was only seven years old when he started the Red Dragon Conservation Team. Its purpose was to protect the tropical rain forest. It has since become an international group of kids who want to save the planet. The kids collect community donations and send them to the Center for Ecosystem Survival (CES) in California. CES uses the donations to buy land in the rain forest and in coral reefs around the world. This protects the land and sea nearby from being destroyed by humans.

Underline text evidence in paragraph 1 that shows how Katie got her idea to help others. Then circle evidence in paragraph 2 that shows what the Red Dragon Conservation Team does.

COLLABORATE

Talk with a partner about how Katie and Evan's organizations are alike and different. Make marks in the margin beside the things both groups have in common. Write the similarities here.

_____

_____

? How does the author use what other young people have done to help you see how you can make a difference?

COLLABORATE

Talk About It Reread paragraph 2 on page 77 and paragraph 1 on page 78. Talk with a partner about how kids can volunteer.

Cite Text Evidence How does the author help you see that you can make a difference, too? Write text evidence in the chart.

What Kids Can Do	What Katie Does	I See That

Write The author uses real life examples of young people who volunteer to ___

_____

_____

QUICK TIP

When I reread, I can use examples the author gives to help me understand the information.

? How is the way the artist shows community similar to the authors' ideas about community in *Aguinaldo* or "Partaking in Public Service"?

COLLABORATE

Talk About It Look at the illustration and read the caption. Talk about what you see happening. Choose some of the people and talk about how you know how they feel about helping.

Cite Text Evidence Circle clues in the illustration that show how people participate in their community in different ways. Then underline ways that they are helping each other. Think about how the characters in *Aguinaldo* and the real-life kids in "Partaking in Public Service" help you understand the meaning of community.

Write The artist's idea of community is like _____

_____

_____

_____

_____

QUICK TIP

I see people helping and participating in a community event. This will help me compare the illustration with the selections I read this week.

ImageZoo/SuperStock

This is an illustration of 12 community members participating in a charity walk in their local park.

Delivering Justice

? How does the author help you visualize how Westley and Grandma were treated at Levy's?

*Literature Anthology:
pages 216–233*

COLLABORATE

Talk About It Reread the second and third paragraphs on page 219. Talk to your partner about what happened to Westley and Grandma at Levy's.

Cite Text Evidence What words does the author use to help you picture what happened? Write text evidence here.

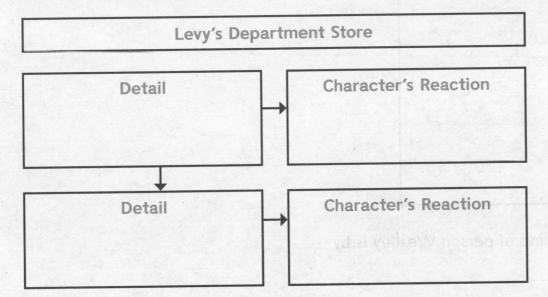

Levy's Department Store

| Detail | → | Character's Reaction |
| Detail | → | Character's Reaction |

Write The author helps me see how Westley and Grandma were treated at

Levy's by _____

_____

CLOSE READING

Tip of the Week

When I **reread**, I can think about how the author uses details to describe an event to help me understand the characters' motives. I use text evidence to answer questions.

Sebastian

Medioimages/Photodisc/Getty Images

? **How do you know what kind of person Westley is?**

COLLABORATE

Talk About It Reread the last paragraph on page 223. Turn to your partner and talk about Westley's role in voter registration.

Cite Text Evidence What do Westley's actions show about his character? Cite text evidence in the chart.

How Westley Helps	What This Shows

Write The author helps me understand what kind of person Westley is by _____

_____

_____

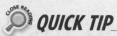

? **How does the illustration help you understand what a boycott is?**

Talk About It Look at the illustration on page 228. Reread page 229. Talk to a partner about what the people are doing.

Cite Text Evidence What clues in the illustration and the text help you understand what a boycott is? Write evidence in the chart.

Illustration Clues	Text Clues	How They Help

Write The author uses the illustration to help me understand that a boycott is

_____

_____

_____

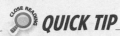 **QUICK TIP**

When I reread, I can use illustrations to help me understand the text.

Your Turn

How does Jim Haskins use the events in Westley's life to show how they contribute to him becoming a leader in his community? Use these sentence frames to help organize your text evidence.

Jim Haskins tells about Westley's boyhood to show . . .

He tells about how Westley . . .

Westley became a leader because . . .

Go Digital!
Write your response online.

Keeping Freedom in the Family: Coming of Age in the Civil Rights Movement

1   As I held on to my father's hand, we joined the line of people chanting and walking back and forth in a picket line in front of Lawrence Hospital. The year was 1965, and the hospital workers needed more money and better working conditions. So there we were on a cold Saturday afternoon to protest. When I looked up, I saw soldiers on the roof of the hospital. I squeezed Daddy's hand a little tighter. The soldiers were there to protect us, he said. We were American citizens, and we had the right to gather and to protest. I raised my picket sign as high as I could. I wasn't afraid. I had Daddy and the American Constitution to protect me.

Reread and use the prompts to take notes in the text.

Circle words that describe the picket line.

Underline why Nora and her family are participating in the protest. Write the reason here:

_____

_____

COLLABORATE

Talk with a partner about how Nora feels. Draw a box around text evidence that supports your ideas.

Siede Preis/Photodisc/Getty Images

1 When four black girls were killed in a church bombing in Alabama, we realized that the fight for change would be hard, long, and dangerous. Mom and Dad encouraged us to think about how we could protest the bombing. Some people said we should boycott Christmas. This was our first Christmas in the new house, and the spirit of giving was important to us.

2 So instead of boycotting Christmas, our family decided to boycott Christmas shopping. Instead of buying gifts, our family gave the money to civil rights groups. Guy, La Verne, and I gave each other gifts we had made with our own hands. And when the time came to hang the home-made paper holiday chain, I wrote the names of the girls in the last four loops. In our own small way, we learned the true meaning of giving.

3 When we gathered for dinner that night, we said a special prayer for the girls and for our country—and I knew that Christmas at the Davis house would never be the same.

Siede Preis/Photodisc/Getty Images

Reread paragraph 1. Underline how the author helps you understand that protesting the bombing was important to her family. Then, in paragraph 2, circle how Nora and her family chose to protest.

COLLABORATE

Reread paragraph 3. Talk with a partner about why "Christmas at the Davis house would never be the same." Make marks in the margin beside the text evidence that supports this.

How does the author help you visualize what it was like for her and her family to walk the picket line?

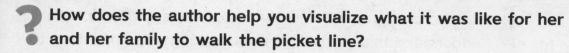
Talk About It Reread the excerpt on page 84. Talk with a partner about what happened at the protest.

Cite Text Evidence What words help you picture how walking the picket line felt to Nora? Write text evidence in the web.

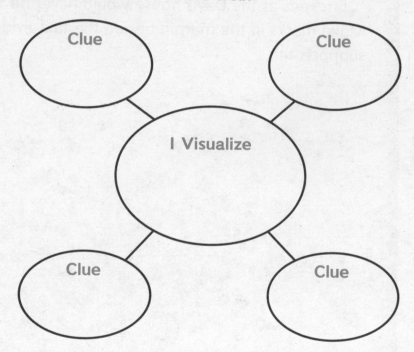

Clue

Clue

I Visualize

Clue

Clue

Write I can visualize what the picket line was like because the author _____

_____

_____

Siede Preis/Photodisc/Getty Images

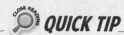
QUICK TIP
When I reread, I use the author's description to help me visualize an important event in the selection.

COLLABORATE

? How does the way Henry Wadsworth Longfellow describe the events of Paul Revere's ride similar to the way the authors of *Delivering Justice* and "Keeping Freedom in the Family" show how one person can make a difference?

Talk About It With a partner, read the poem. Talk about what Paul Revere plans to do.

Cite Text Evidence Circle words and phrases that describe the details of Paul Revere's plan. Underline the phrase that shows how Paul Revere took action and made a difference that night.

Write Henry Wadsworth Longfellow's description is like _____

_____

_____

_____

_____

_____

George Doyle/SuperStock

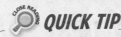

QUICK TIP

I can use the way Henry Wadsworth Longfellow uses words and phrases to describe Paul Revere's plan. This will help me compare the poem to the selections I read this week.

from *Paul Revere's Ride*

He said to his friend, "If the British march
By land or sea from the town to-night,
Hang a lantern aloft in the belfry-arch
Of the North-Church-tower, as a signal-light,—
One if by land, and two if by sea;
And I on the opposite shore will be,
Ready to ride and spread the alarm
Through every Middlesex village and farm,
For the country-folk to be up and to arm."

— Henry Wadsworth Longfellow

Abe's Honest Words: The Life of Abraham Lincoln

Literature Anthology: pages 240–259

? How does the author help you visualize what Abraham Lincoln saw in New Orleans?

COLLABORATE

Talk About It Reread the last two paragraphs on page 244. Turn to your partner and describe what Lincoln saw in New Orleans.

Cite Text Evidence How does the author's description and Lincoln's own words help paint a vivid picture of what Lincoln saw? Cite text evidence in the chart.

Author's Description	Lincoln's Words	What I Visualize

Write The author helps me visualize what Lincoln saw in New Orleans by _____

_____

_____

CLOSE READING
Tip of the Week

When I **reread**, I can think about how the author uses words and phrases. I look for text evidence to answer questions.

Drew

Paul Bradbury/OJO Images/Getty Images

? **How does the author use Lincoln's quotation to help you understand why people liked him?**

COLLABORATE

Talk About It Reread Lincoln's quotation on page 247. Turn to your partner and talk about how he describes himself.

Cite Text Evidence What do Lincoln's words tell people about him? Cite text evidence.

Lincoln's Words	What They Show

Write The author uses Lincoln's quotation because it _____

_____

_____

QUICK TIP

When I reread, I can look at how the author uses first person accounts to help me understand more about a person.

How do you know how Lincoln feels about ending slavery?

COLLABORATE

Talk About It Reread paragraph 2 and Lincoln's quotation on page 257. Turn to your partner and discuss the words Lincoln uses to express how he feels about slavery.

Cite Text Evidence How does Lincoln's quotation help you understand his feelings about slavery? Write text evidence and explain how it helps.

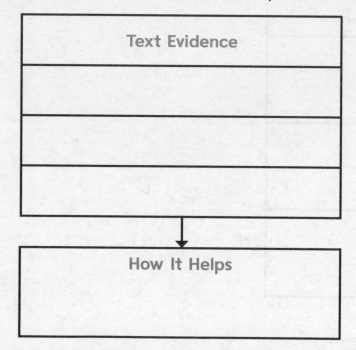

Text Evidence

How It Helps

Write I know how Lincoln feels about slavery because he _____

_____

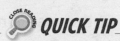
QUICK TIP

As I reread, I can use primary sources to help me understand a person's point of view.

Your Turn

Do you think the author's use of Abraham Lincoln's quotes throughout this selection helps you understand the events that lead to change? Use these sentence frames to organize your text evidence.

The author uses Lincoln's quotes to . . .

They also tell me about . . .

This helps me understand how . . .

Go Digital!
Write your response online.

A New Birth of Freedom

---

1   The Battle of Gettysburg, Pennsylvania, in July 1863 was a turning point in the Civil War. Thousands of soldiers on both sides lost their lives. After the battle, a proclamation created a national cemetery there. President Lincoln came to Gettysburg on November 19, 1863 to honor the soldiers who had died. In his address, Lincoln praised their courage and asked people to honor them by working toward a "new birth of freedom." At the time, reactions to his speech were mixed. It has since become one of the most famous speeches in our nation's history.

The Gettysburg Address

2   Four score and seven years ago our fathers brought forth on this continent, a new nation, conceived in liberty, and dedicated to the proposition that all men are created equal.

Reread and use the prompts to take notes in the text.

Underline how you know that the Battle of Gettysburg was an important battle in our country's history. Circle why President Lincoln went to Gettysburg when it was over. Write the reason here:

_____

_____

COLLABORATE

Talk with a partner about how the words Lincoln uses in the beginning of "The Gettysburg Address" help you understand the importance of Lincoln's speech. Draw a box around the strong words Lincoln uses to open his speech.

3   Now we are engaged in a great civil war, testing whether that nation, or any nation so conceived and so dedicated, can long endure. We are met on a great battlefield of that war. We have come to dedicate a portion of that field, as a final resting place for those who here gave their lives, that that nation might live. It is altogether fitting and proper that we should do this.

4   But, in a larger sense, we cannot dedicate – we cannot consecrate – we cannot hallow – this ground. The brave men, living and dead, who struggled here, have consecrated it, far above our poor power to add or detract. The world will little note, nor long remember what we say here, but it can never forget what they did here.

Reread paragraphs 3 and 4. Underline phrases that tell you this is a first-person statement. What was Lincoln's purpose for making this speech? Circle the text evidence and write it here:

_____

_____

_____

COLLABORATE

Talk with a partner about how Lincoln feels about the men who fought for their country at Gettysburg. How does he inspire his listeners? Make marks in the margin beside text evidence that supports your discussion.

? How does the author's use of a first-person statement help you understand how President Lincoln felt about the soldiers who fought during the Civil War?

COLLABORATE

Talk About It With a partner, reread the excerpts on pages 91–92. Use your annotations to talk about how the speech and the author's introduction help you understand how important the Battle of Gettysburg was.

Cite Text Evidence What words and phrases help you understand how Lincoln felt about the soldiers who fought? Write text evidence in the chart.

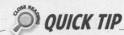
Author's Description	Lincoln's Speech	What I Understand

Write The author uses Lincoln's speech to help me _____

_____

_____

How does the artist use realistic details in the same way as the authors of *Abe's Honest Words* and "A New Birth of Freedom" to help you understand how words lead to change?

**QUICK TIP**

I can use details in the painting to help me understand the importance of the Founding Fathers' task. This will help me compare text to art.

COLLABORATE

Talk About It Look at the painting. Talk with a partner about the details that show what Benjamin Franklin, John Adams, and Thomas Jefferson are doing.

Cite Text Evidence Circle clues in the painting that help you understand how the Founding Fathers wrote the Declaration of Independence. Draw a box around details that show that it wasn't an easy thing for them to do. Read the caption. Underline text evidence that helps you understand more about how the Founding Fathers wrote the document.

Write The artist's realistic details in the painting are like _____

_____

_____

_____

This painting by Jean Leon Gerome Ferris depicts Benjamin Franklin, John Adams, and Thomas Jefferson drafting the Declaration of Independence in 1776.

John Parrot/Stocktrek Images/Getty Images

A New Kind of Corn

Literature Anthology:
pages 264–267

? Why does the author use the pie chart to show how corn is used?

COLLABORATE

Talk About It Reread the last paragraph on page 265. With a partner, analyze the pie chart. Talk about how the information in the chart is related to the text.

Cite Text Evidence In what ways does the information in the text and the pie chart help you understand more about Bt corn? Find evidence and write it in the chart.

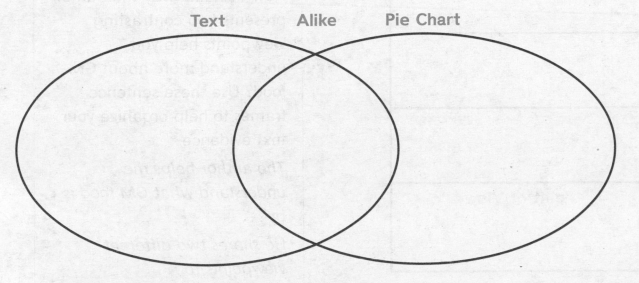

Text   Alike   Pie Chart

Tip of the **Week**
CLOSE READING

When I **reread**, I can look at how the author uses text features to help me understand more about the topic. I look for text evidence to answer questions.

Cristina

Write The author's purpose for using the pie chart is to _____

_____

_____

? **How do the authors of both persuasive articles help you understand what they think?**

COLLABORATE

Talk About It Reread the two articles on pages 266 and 267. Turn to a partner and talk about the two different perspectives presented in the article.

Cite Text Evidence What clues help you understand the points of view of the farmer and the consumer? Write text evidence in the chart.

Bt Corn Is Better	Bt Corn Could Be Bad
Point of View	Point of View

Write The authors of the persuasive articles help me understand what they

think by _____

_____

QUICK TIP

I can use these sentence frames when we talk about the two different perspectives.

The farmer explains that planting Bt corn has . . .

The consumer explains that Bt corn . . .

Your Turn

How does the way the author presents two contrasting viewpoints help you understand more about GM food? Use these sentence frames to help organize your text evidence.

The author helps me understand what GM food is by . . .

He shares two different viewpoints to . . .

This helps me understand that GM food . . .

Go Digital!
Write your response online.

The Pick of the Patch

[1]   This world record-breaking pumpkin tipped the scales at more than 1,810 pounds. What is the secret to growing a giant gourd? According to record-breaker Chris Stevens, "Sunshine, rain, cow manure, fish [fertilizer], and seaweed." Read on for a recipe you can recreate at home.

[2]   Growing a giant pumpkin takes knowledge and skill. Follow these six simple steps to grow your own great gourd.

1. Study up on seeds.

Some popular pumpkin seeds that get big results include Prizewinner Hybrid, Atlantic Giant, Mammoth Gold, and Big Max. Many are sold online for just $1.

2. Take your time.

Giant pumpkins need time to grow. May is a good month to plant seeds in a pot. Let them make advancements in that safe space before you transplant them outside. Plant them in good quality soil and fertilize them well.

Reread and use the prompts to take notes in the text.

In paragraph 1, underline how the author gets you interested in reading more about how to grow a giant pumpkin.

Reread paragraph 2. Circle what it takes to grow a great gourd. Write it here:

1. _____

2. _____

3. _____

COLLABORATE

Talk with a partner about how the author helps you understand how to grow a giant pumpkin. Draw a box around how he helps you understand what each step is going to be about.

? How does the way the author organizes the information in this selection help you understand what it takes to grow a great pumpkin?

Talk About It Reread the excerpt on page 97. Talk with a partner about what you learned from the author about how to get started growing a big pumpkin.

Cite Text Evidence What does the author use to help you understand how a pumpkin can grow to be 1,810 pounds? Write text evidence in the chart.

What the Author Does	How It Helps

Write The author helps me understand how to grow a great pumpkin by _____

_____

_____

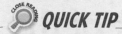

QUICK TIP

I can use these sentence frames when we talk about what we learned about growing a giant pumpkin.

First, the author uses a quotation to . . .

Then, the author lists . . .

? How is the way the songwriter organizes the song like the way the authors use organization in "A New Kind of Corn" and "The Pick of the Patch" to show point of view?

CLOSE READING
QUICK TIP

I see how the songwriter organizes the lyrics to show point of view. This will help me compare the song to texts.

COLLABORATE

Talk About It Read the lyrics of the song. Talk about how the writer shows that there are two points of view.

Cite Text Evidence Circle the lyrics that show one point of view. Then underline the phrases that show the other point of view. Think about how the authors of the selections you read this week use organization to share point of view.

Write The songwriter organizes the information like _____

_____

_____

_____

_____

"Did You Feed My Cow"
(lyrics)

Did you feed my cow?
(Yes, Ma-am)

Could you tell me how?
(Yes, Ma-am)

What did you feed her?
(Corn and Hay)

What did you feed her?
(Corn and Hay)

Did you milk her good?
(Yes, Ma-am)

Now did you milk her like you should?
(Yes, Ma-am)

How did you milk her?
(Squish, Squish, Squish)

How did you milk her?
(Squish, Squish, Squish)

See How They Run

 How does the author help you understand what the Founding Fathers did?

Literature Anthology: pages 270–281

COLLABORATE

Talk About It Reread page 273. Turn and talk to your partner about how George Washington and the Founding Fathers created our American government.

Cite Text Evidence What examples show how the Founding Fathers used ideas from Greek and Roman governments? Write text evidence in the chart.

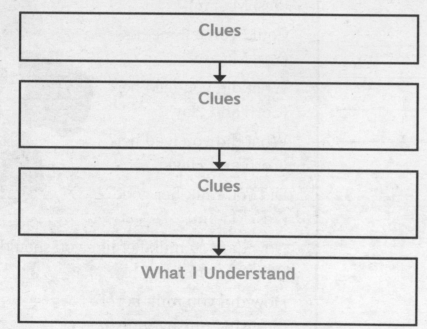

Clues

↓

Clues

↓

Clues

↓

What I Understand

 **Tip** of the **Week**

When I **reread**, I can think about how the author uses words and phrases. I look for text evidence to answer questions.

Malia

Write The author helps me understand what the Founding Fathers did by _____

_____

_____

? **Why does the author include Ben Franklin's quote in the sidebar?**

COLLABORATE

Talk About It Reread the sidebar on page 274. Turn and talk with a partner about what Ben Franklin said.

Cite Text Evidence What words and phrases help you understand Ben Franklin's message? Write text evidence in the chart.

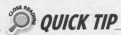
QUICK TIP

I can use these sentence frames when we talk about what Ben Franklin said.

The author helps me understand what Ben Franklin said by . . .

This author uses this quote to show . . .

Text Evidence	Author's Purpose

Write The author includes Ben Franklin's quote to _____

_____

_____

? Why does the author give specific, real life examples of kids as leaders?

COLLABORATE

Talk About It Reread page 279. Turn to your partner and talk about how Shadia Wood helped her community.

Cite Text Evidence What words and phrases show what Shadia did to help her community? Write text evidence in the chart.

What Shadia Did	How It Helped	Author's Purpose

Write The author gives examples of real life examples of kids as leaders

to _____

_____

_____

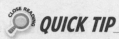
QUICK TIP
When I reread, I can use text evidence to understand the author's purpose.

Your Turn

What is Susan E. Goodman's viewpoint about democracy and our right to vote? Use these sentence frames to organize your text evidence.

Susan E. Goodman tells how the Founding Fathers . . .

She describes how democracy . . .

This helps me understand that she . . .

Go Digital!
Write your response online.

The Birth of American Democracy

1   Every Fourth of July, Americans celebrate the birthday of the United States. Fireworks and parades remind us that the thirteen colonies declared independence from Great Britain on July 4, 1776. That birthday took place in Philadelphia, Pennsylvania. There, the Second Continental Congress approved the Declaration of Independence. This document formed a new nation, the United States of America. The Declaration is almost like our country's original birthday card.

Our Founding Fathers

2   Five men, including John Adams, Thomas Jefferson, and Benjamin Franklin, wrote the Declaration of Independence. Jefferson wrote the first draft. His famous words sum up a basic American belief – "all men are created equal."

Reread and use the prompts to take notes in the text.

Underline two details in paragraph 1 that explain why the Fourth of July is called America's birthday. Circle words and phrases that help you understand why we celebrate.

COLLABORATE

Talk with a partner about how the author describes the Declaration of Independence. Draw a box around the text evidence.

Why does the author include Thomas Jefferson's famous words? Make a mark in the margin beside the text evidence Write it here:

_____

_____

[3] The men who signed the Declaration are called the Founding Fathers of our country. Signing the Declaration put the founders' lives in danger. They knew that their signatures made them traitors to Great Britain. They also knew that, if the colonies won the war, their names would go down in history.

[4] Led by General George Washington, the colonists fought passionately for their freedom. After a long, bloody war, the British surrendered in 1781, and a peace treaty was signed in 1783. Our new nation was still a work in progress, however. Americans disagreed about how much power a federal, or central, government should have. Given that they had just won freedom from a powerful British king, Americans did not want their government to have too much power.

Reread the excerpt. Underline how the author helps you understand how signing the Declaration of Independence was both risky and positive for the Founding Fathers. Write text evidence here:

1. _____

2. _____

COLLABORATE

Reread paragraph 4. Talk with a partner about how the author shows how the colonists felt about freedom. Circle text evidence.

? **Why is "The Birth of American Democracy" a good title for this selection?**

COLLABORATE

Talk About It Reread the excerpts on pages 103 and 104. Talk about why the Fourth of July is such an important holiday.

Cite Text Evidence What words and phrases show how our government was created? Write text evidence in the chart.

Text Evidence	Author's Purpose

Write "The Birth of American Democracy" is a good title because _____

_____

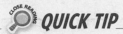
QUICK TIP

When I reread, I can use headings to help me understand how the author organizes information.

? How does the songwriter help you understand his point of view and how is it similar to the way the authors of *See How They Run* and "The Birth of American Democracy" help you know how they feel?

Talk About It Tarriers are people who waste time. In the song, the tarriers are the railroad workers who can't work quickly enough to meet the foreman's demands. Read the lyrics. Talk with a partner about how the songwriter helps you visualize what Jerry McCann was like.

Cite Text Evidence Circle words and phrases in the lyrics that show how the songwriter feels about Jerry McCann. Underline what Jerry McCann says.

Write The songwriter and authors show how they feel by _____

_____

_____

_____

QUICK TIP

I can use how the songwriter helps me understand how he feels about a character. This will help me compare the song to the selections I read this week.

from Drill, Ye Tarriers

Now, our new foreman was Jerry McCann,

You can bet that he was sure a blame mean man,

Last week a premature blast went off,

And a mile in the air went big Jim Goff,

Now, next time payday come around,

Jim Goff a dollar short was found,

When asked what for, came this reply,

"You were docked for the time you were up in the sky!"

Datacraft Co Ltd/Getty Images

LaRue for Mayor

? **How does the author use Ike's letters to add humor to the story?**

COLLABORATE

Talk About It Reread page 293. Talk with a partner about what Ike writes in his letter and what you see in the illustration.

Cite Text Evidence What clues from the letter and illustration add humor to the story? Write evidence in the chart.

Illustration Clues	Text Evidence	What This Shows

Write The author uses Ike's letter to add humor to the story by _____

_____

Literature Anthology: pages 288–307

CLOSE READING **Tip of the Week**

When I **reread**, I can use clues from the illustration to help me understand a character's actions. I look for text evidence to answer questions.

Ricky

? **How does the author use the newspaper article to reveal more about Bugwort's character?**

Talk About It Reread page 295. Turn to a partner and talk about what Bugwort says about dogs.

Cite Text Evidence What words and phrases show what Bugwort is proposing? Write text evidence and tell what Bugwort is like.

Text Evidence	Bugwort

Write The author uses the newspaper article to show that Bugwort _____

_____

_____

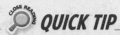 **QUICK TIP**

I can use these sentence frames when we talk about Bugwort.

The author shows that Bugwort wants to . . .

This helps me see that he is . . .

How do Ike's dog characteristics add humor to the story?

COLLABORATE

Talk About It Reread page 301 and look at the illustration. Turn to your partner and talk about what Ike says and how he changes the poster.

Cite Text Evidence What are some funny things Ike says and does? Write text evidence in the chart.

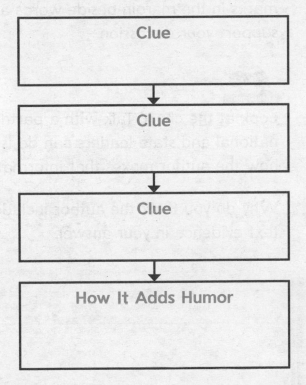

Clue

↓

Clue

↓

Clue

↓

How It Adds Humor

Write Ike's dog characteristics adds humor to the story by _____

_____

 QUICK TIP

When I reread, I can think about how the author uses humor.

Your Turn

How does the author use letters and newspaper articles to develop the characters of Ike and Bugwort? Use these sentence frames to organize your text evidence.

The author uses letters to . . .

The newspaper articles help me . . .

The author develops the characters by . . .

Go Digital!
Write your response online.

Bringing Government Home

1   National, state, and local governments share the same basic structure. The executive, legislative, and judicial branches make up the three branches of government. Each branch of government has specific duties and powers. These powers differ in national and state governments.

The Executive Branch

2   The President is the leader of the national executive branch. Similarly, a governor heads up each state executive branch. The governor makes important decisions about the state. Each state has its own structure and set of officials who are below the governor.

Just a Few National Powers Versus State Powers

National Leaders Can ...
- Print money
- Declare war
- Enforce the U.S. Constitution

State Leaders Can ...
- Issue licenses
- Provide for public health and safety
- Amend state constitutions

Reread and use the prompts to take notes in the text.

Underline words in paragraph 1 that show how national and state governments are alike.

Reread the rest of the excerpt. How does the heading help you know what the next section is about? Make marks in the margin beside words and phrases to support your discussion.

COLLABORATE

Look at the chart. Talk with a partner about how what national and state leaders can do is different. Circle how the author makes that information clear.

Why do you think the author includes the chart? Use text evidence in your answer.

_____

_____

(l) Chip Somodevilla/Getty Images News/Getty Images; (r) Mel Curtis/Photonica/Getty Images

The Legislative Branch

[1]   State legislatures also have strong leaders called senators and representatives. These members try to improve their state by passing new laws. Senator Anthony C. Hill worked hard for the state of Florida. He helped to create and pass new laws. As a legislator, Hill worked to pass important civil rights legislation. He also improved African American voter turnout in Florida elections. In addition, Hill helped to increase the state's minimum wage and reduce class sizes in schools.

[2]   Local legislators can create similar results in their counties, cities, and towns. They may pass laws that relate to parks, public transportation, and police departments, to name a few.

In paragraph 1, circle words that show how the author feels about state leaders.

Reread paragraph 2 and underline the sentence that compares state and local legislators. Write it here:

_____

_____

COLLABORATE

Talk with a partner about Senator Anthony C. Hill. Make marks in the margin beside the things he has done.

? **How does the author's use of real examples help you understand what senators do?**

COLLABORATE

Talk About It Reread the excerpt on page 111. Talk with a partner about Senator Hill.

Cite Text Evidence What words and phrases help you understand what Senator Hill has done? Write text evidence in the chart.

Text Evidence	How It Helps

Write The author's use of real examples helps me understand _____

_____

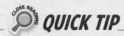
QUICK TIP

When I reread, I can think about how the author uses real life examples to help me understand a topic.

? How is the way the artist portrays the election process similar to the portrayal of the election process in *LaRue for Mayor* and "Bringing Government Home"?

 QUICK TIP

I can see the election process in the painting. This will help me compare art to text.

COLLABORATE

Talk About It Look at George Caleb Bingham's painting and read the caption. With a partner, discuss what you see. Choose some of the people and talk about what they are doing.

Cite Text Evidence Draw a box around the candidate. Circle clues in the painting that show what goes on during an election. Think about how this painting is like the election process in the selections you read this week.

Write I understand the election process because the artist and authors _____

_____

_____

_____

Yale University Art Gallery

This is a black and white print of an original painting by American artist George Caleb Bingham. The painting, *Stump Speaking*, was painted in the 1850s. It shows a large group of community members gathered to talk with a candidate.

The Moon Over Star

Literature Anthology:
pages 314–329

? How does the author help you understand how Gramps feels about the moon landing on television?

COLLABORATE

Talk About It Reread page 320. Turn to a partner and discuss Gramps's reaction to the moon landing on television.

Cite Text Evidence What words and phrases show how everyone reacts to Gram's announcement? Write text evidence and explain what it shows.

Response to Gram's Announcement	What This Shows

Write I know how Gramps feels about the moon landing because the author

_____

_____

Tip of the **Week**

When I **reread**, I can use the author's words and phrases to help me understand how a character feels. I look for text evidence to answer questions.

Patrice

? **How does the author use words and phrases to help you visualize the summer night's mood?**

COLLABORATE

Talk About It Reread page 324. Talk with a partner about how the author's description of the family's time outside at night makes you feel.

Cite Text Evidence What phrases help you picture what that night was like? Write text evidence in the chart.

QUICK TIP

I can use these sentence frames when we talk about mood.

The author describes the night . . .

This helps me feel . . .

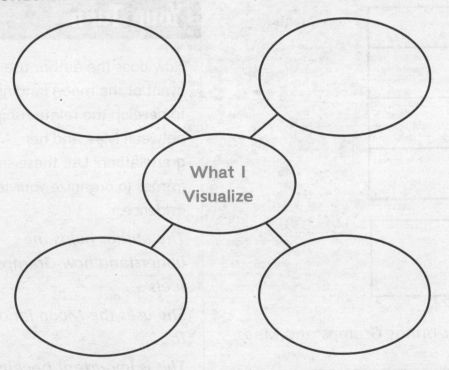

What I Visualize

Write I can visualize the summer night's mood because the author _____

_____

_____

How does the moonwalk bring Gramps and Mae closer together?

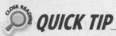 **QUICK TIP**

As I reread, I pay attention to the characters' words and actions. This helps me understand their feelings and motivations.

COLLABORATE

Talk About It Reread the last paragraph on page 326. Turn to a partner and talk about how Gramps reacts to what the family is watching on television.

Cite Text Evidence What does Gramps say and do? Write text evidence and tell what it helps you understand.

Text Evidence

↓

What I Understand

Write The author helps me see how the moonwalk brings Gramps and Mae closer together by _____

_____

_____

Your Turn

How does the author use the event of the moon landing to develop the relationship between Mae and her grandfather? Use these sentence frames to organize your text evidence.

The author helps me understand how Gramps feels . . .

She uses the Moon landing to . . .

This is important because at the end of the story . . .

Go Digital!
Write your response online.

3...2...1 We Have Spin-Off!

All Around Us

1   Actually, space is not far away. It's all around us. The technology used in the space program has led to many products that people and businesses use every day. These improvements and inventions are called spin-offs from the space program. Today's lightweight athletic shoes use padding and air cushion soles first used in space suits. Space program scientists developed cordless appliances and dried foods for astronauts. School bus frames, brakes, and tires are safer today because they use technology first developed for spacecraft.

2   Many spin-offs are currently found in homes. Smoke detectors were developed decades ago for use on Skylab, America's first space station. Cordless tools were developed to bring back rock samples from the moon. Do you ever talk to other players over headsets during online video games? If so, you are using a spin-off from the headset that astronaut Neil Armstrong spoke into when he made his "giant leap" onto the moon.

Reread and use the prompts to take notes in the text.

Underline the sentence in paragraph 1 that tells why space is all around us. Then circle examples of how the author supports that statement.

COLLABORATE

Reread paragraph 2. Talk with a partner about more spin-offs of the space program. Circle three more examples and write them here:

1. _____

2. _____

3. _____

Sports

1. Spin-offs have also changed sports for athletes and for fans. Helmets for football players use padding first developed for spacecraft seats. Many athletes use heart rate monitors when they work out. Those were first developed to keep track of an astronaut's health during long flights.

2. Spin-offs help fans, too. Many stadiums have roofs that cover the field during bad weather. The fabric used in those roofs was first used in astronauts' spacesuits. Those large plasma screens that show game action were also first developed for the space program.

Reread the excerpt. Underline words and phrases that show how spin-offs help athletes and fans. Then go back and circle how each invention came from the space program.

Talk with a partner about why "Sports" is a good heading for this section. Make marks in the margin beside text evidence to support your answer. Write it here:

_____

_____

_____

? How does the author help you understand what he means by the sentence, "It's all around us?"

 **QUICK TIP**

When I reread, I can find text evidence to support statements the author makes.

COLLABORATE

Talk About It Reread the excerpt on page 117. Talk with a partner about what a spin-off is.

Cite Text Evidence What words and phrases show that spin-offs are all around us? Write text evidence in the chart.

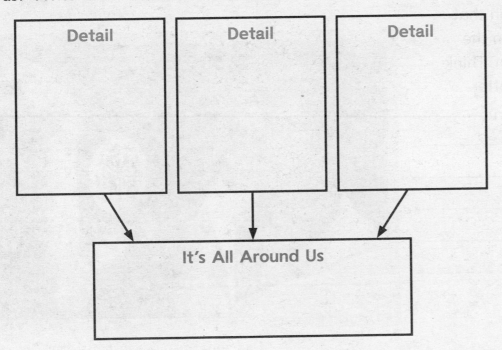

| Detail | Detail | Detail |

It's All Around Us

Write The author helps me understand what "It's all around us" means by

_____

_____

_____

How do the photographer and the authors of *The Moon Over Star* and "3...2...1 We Have Spin-Off!" help you understand that technology really is all around us?

COLLABORATE

Talk About It Read the caption and look at the photograph. Talk with a partner about what Claudia Mitchell is able to do with her new prosthetic arm.

Cite Text Evidence Circle clues in the photograph that shows what Claudia can do. Underline evidence in the caption that shows how she controls her new arm. Think about how technology has made Claudia's life better.

Write I understand that technology is all around us because the photographer and authors _____

_____

_____

_____

 **QUICK TIP**

I see a woman using a bionic arm. I can think about why this moment is important. This will help me compare the photo to the texts.

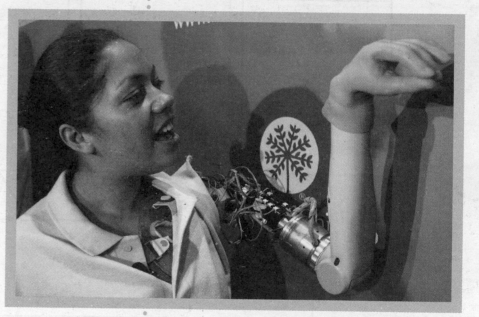

Win McNamee/Getty Images News/Getty Images

In 2006, Claudia Mitchell was the first woman to receive a thought-controlled bionic arm. If she wants to pick something up, all she has to do is think about what she wants her prosthesis to do, and it does what she thinks.

Why Does the Moon Change Shape?

Literature Anthology:
pages 336–349

? How does the author use diagrams and captions to help you understand the phases of the Moon?

COLLABORATE

Talk About It Look at the diagram and reread the caption on page 339. Talk with a partner about the phases of the Moon.

Cite Text Evidence What clues in the diagram and caption explain the phases of the Moon? Write evidence here.

CLOSE READING

Tip of the Week

When I **reread**, I can use diagrams and captions to help me understand text. I look for text evidence to answer questions.

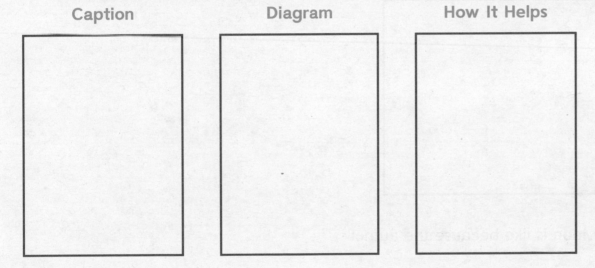

Caption	Diagram	How It Helps

Jason

Write The author's use of the diagram and caption helps me understand _____

_____

_____

Echo/Cultura/Getty Images

? **How do the author's words help you understand what the First Quarter Moon is like?**

COLLABORATE

Talk About It Reread the last three paragraphs on page 347. Talk with a partner about what the First Quarter Moon looks like.

Cite Text Evidence How does the author describe the First Quarter Moon? Write text evidence in the chart.

Text Evidence	How It Helps

Write I understand what the First Quarter Moon is like because the author

_____

_____

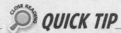 **QUICK TIP**

I can use these sentence frames when we talk about the First Quarter Moon.

The author says the First Quarter Moon is . . .

This helps me understand that . . .

? **Why is *Why Does the Moon Change Shape?* a good title for this selection?**

COLLABORATE

Talk About It Reread page 348. Talk with a partner about how the Moon changes shape.

Cite Text Evidence How does the author organize the information? Write text evidence and tell how it helps you understand how the Moon changes shape.

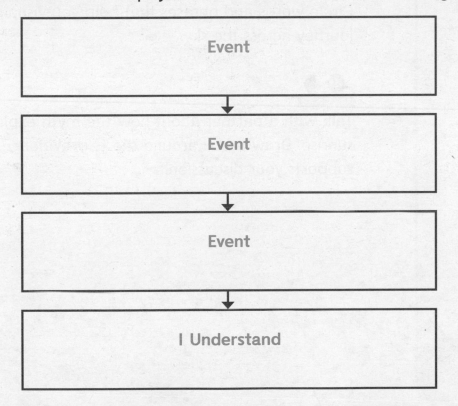

Event

↓

Event

↓

Event

↓

I Understand

Write *Why Does the Moon Change Shape?* is a good title because _____

_____

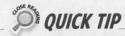

QUICK TIP

I can use the author's words and phrases to help visualize how the Moon changes shape.

Your Turn

How does Melissa Stewart help you understand how the Moon changes? Use these sentence frames to help organize your text evidence.

Melissa Stewart uses text features to . . .

She also uses cause and effect to explain . . .

This helps me understand . . .

Go Digital!
Write your response online.

How It Came to Be

Why the Sun Travels Across the Sky

A retelling of a Greek myth

1   Helios, the Titan god of the sun, brings light to the earth. He dwells in a golden palace in the east on the river Okeanos. Each morning, Helios follows his sister Eos, the goddess of the Dawn, across the sky. He drives a shining chariot, drawn by four noble steeds, upward through the clouds. The chariot moves higher as rays of brilliant light pour forth from Helios's crown. Slowly, the steeds climb with a single purpose. Hours later, they finally reach the highest point of the sky.

Reread and use the prompts to take notes in the text.

Underline what Helios's purpose is each day. Write it here:

_____

Circle words and phrases that help you visualize Helios's journey across the sky.

COLLABORATE

Talk with a partner about how the myth explains the sunrise. Draw a box around the text evidence that supports your discussion.

2   Pausing only briefly to rest, Helios then begins the long and difficult journey downward. He travels toward his western palace. The path is steep and treacherous. Helios must master his steeds so that they do not fall headlong into the earth. If his chariot happened to drop too low in the sky, it would scorch the land and all its people.

3   After many hours, Helios arrives safely at the gates of his western palace. As darkness overtakes the earth, he begins his journey back to the east. Instead of traveling across the sky, he and his steeds sail in a golden boat from the gods along the river Okeanos. He returns to his eastern palace to repeat his journey across the sky.

4   Helios will continue to take this journey for as long as there are days and nights. His shining light warms us each day as the sun travels tirelessly across the sky.

Circle words and phrases in paragraph 2 that show how dangerous the journey downward is.

COLLABORATE

Reread paragraph 3. Talk with a partner about how the myth explains the sunrise and sunset. Discuss how Helios's travels correspond to the rising and setting of the sun. Make marks in the margin beside text evidence. Write it here:

_____

_____

Underline the clue in paragraph 4 that shows how people feel about Helios and his journey.

? How does the author use words and phrases to help you understand how people felt about the gods?

COLLABORATE

Talk About It Reread paragraph 4 on page 125. Talk with a partner about what Helios does every day.

Cite Text Evidence What sentence shows how people felt about Helios? Write text evidence here.

Text Evidence	How People Felt

Write The author helps me understand how people felt about the gods by

_____

_____

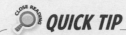
QUICK TIP

When I reread, I can use the author's words and phrases to understand point of view.

? How does the way the artist structured the print similar to the way the authors organized text in *Why Does the Moon Change Shape?* and "How It Came to Be"?

🔍 **QUICK TIP**

I can use the way the artist organized the images to help me compare it with the texts I read.

Talk About It Look at the print and read the caption. Talk with a partner about what you see in each panel.

Cite Text Evidence Circle clues in the print that show how the artist feels about the bay. Underline one image in each panel that stands out. Think about why the artist organized his print into three separate sections.

Write Organization in the print and selections helps me _____

_____

_____

_____

Yale University Art Gallery

This is a triptych, or three-paneled woodblock print. It was created by a Japanese painter and printmaker in 1857. "Kanazawa in Moonlight" shows a calm night scene of the Kanazawa Bay in Japan.

Swimming to the Rock

Literature Anthology:
pages 356–358

? How does the poet help you visualize how the narrator feels as she watches her father and brothers swim?

COLLABORATE

Talk About It Reread stanzas 3–5 on pages 356 and 357. Talk with a partner about what the narrator's father and brothers are doing.

Cite Text Evidence What words and phrases show what the narrator sees as she watches them swim? Write text evidence in the chart.

Text Evidence	What I Visualize

Write The poet helps me visualize how the narrator feels by _____

_____

CLOSE READING
Tip of the **Week**

When I **reread**, I think about how the poet uses sensory details to describe how characters feel. I look for text evidence to answer questions.

Alex

The Moondust Footprint

? What words and phrases does the poet use to express the mood and feeling of the narrator?

Talk About It Reread page 358. Talk with a partner about how the narrator describes the Moon landing.

Cite Text Evidence What words and phrases create mood? Write text evidence in the chart.

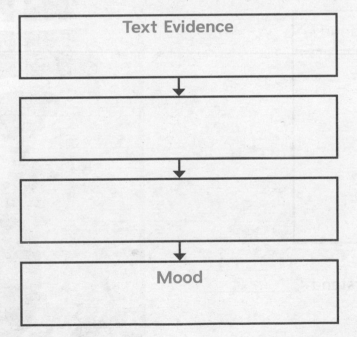

Text Evidence

↓

↓

↓

Mood

Write The poet expresses the mood and feeling of the narrator by _____

QUICK TIP

When I reread, I can think about words and phrases. This helps me understand the poem's mood.

Your Turn

Compare and contrast the narrators' feelings in "Swimming to the Rock" and "The Moondust Footprint." Use these sentence frames to help organize your text evidence.

The narrators of both poems use descriptive language to . . .

This helps me understand the narrator's feelings by . . .

This is important because it helps me understand how . . .

Go Digital!
Write your response online.

Genius

? How does the poet use figurative language to help you understand what the narrator is like?

COLLABORATE

Talk About It Reread the last two stanzas on page 360. Talk with a partner about what the narrator and his sister are doing.

Cite Text Evidence What words and phrases describe the narrator's sister? Write text evidence in the chart.

Figurative Language	What I Understand

Write The poet uses figurative language to help me understand _____

_____

_____

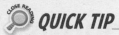

Winner

? How does the poet help you understand how the narrator feels about his father?

Talk About It Reread the last stanza on page 361. Talk with a partner about what the narrator says his dad does when he hits the ball.

Cite Text Evidence What phrases show how the narrator feels about his father? Write text evidence in the chart and tell how it helps you understand.

Text Evidence	How It Helps

Write I know how the narrator feels about his father because the poet

_____

_____

QUICK TIP

I can use these sentence frames when we talk about the narrator's father.

The poet describes how the father reacts by . . .

This helps me understand that the narrator feels . . .

? How does Douglas Malloch's description of success compare to the way the poets use words and phrases to tell what success means in the poems you read this week?

COLLABORATE

Talk About It Read the poem. Talk with a partner about how the poem describes what it means to be a success.

Cite Text Evidence Underline words and phrases that show how the poet describes what success means. Make marks in the margin beside text evidence where the poet is comparing two things.

Write Douglas Malloch and the poets I read this week describe success by _____

_____

_____

QUICK TIP

I can use the poet's words and phrases to understand how he feels about success. This will help me compare the poems.

from

Be the Best of Whatever You Are

We can't all be captains, we've got to be crew,
    There's something for all of us here.
There's big work to do and there's lesser to do,
    And the task we must do is the near.

If you can't be a highway then just be a trail,
    If you can't be the sun be a star;
It isn't by size that you win or you fail—
    Be the best of whatever you are!

— Douglas Malloch

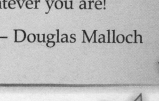

Mama, I'll Give You the World

? How does the author use figurative language to help you understand Mama and Luisa's relationship?

Literature Anthology: pages 362–377

Talk About It Reread the first two paragraphs on page 366. Turn to your partner and talk about how the author describes Mama and Luisa.

Cite Text Evidence What examples of metaphors tell you more about Mama and Luisa? Write text evidence in the chart.

Figurative Language	What does this show?

Write The author uses figurative language to show that _____

_____

_____

Tip of the Week

CLOSE READING

When I **reread**, I can think about how the author compares things. I look for text evidence to answer questions.

Imani

Vanessa Gavalya/Photodisc/Getty Images

? **How does the author emphasize the importance of Mama and Luisa's caring relationship?**

COLLABORATE

Talk About It Reread page 370. Turn to a partner and talk about what Luisa and Mama mean when they say they want to give each other the world.

Cite Text Evidence What words and phrases show that Mama and Luisa care about one another? Write text evidence here.

	What They Think or Say	What They Do
Mama		
Luisa		

Write The author emphasizes the importance of Mama and Luisa's

relationship by _____

_____

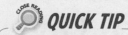
QUICK TIP

I can use these sentence frames when we talk about Mama and Luisa.

Mama wants to give Luisa the world by . . .

Luisa wants to give Mama the world by . . .

? **Why is the illustration of Mama and Luisa an important part of the story?**

Talk About It Reread the last paragraph on page 374. Look at the illustration on page 375. Turn to your partner and talk about how the illustration helps you visualize the moment.

Cite Text Evidence How does the illustration connect to what you read? Write text evidence in the chart.

Illustration Clues	How It Connects

Write The illustration of Mama and Luisa is an important part of the story

because _____

_____

_____

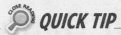 **QUICK TIP**

As I reread, I can think about how the illustration supports the text to answer the question.

Your Turn

Think about how the author focuses on Mama and Luisa's relationship throughout the story. Why is *Mama, I'll Give You the World* a good title for this story? Use these sentence frames to organize your text evidence.

The author shows how Mama and Luisa . . .

The author does this by . . .

The illustrations show . . .

Go Digital!
Write your response online.

What If It Happened to You?

1. "Yasmin and her family are safe, but the Ali family has lost everything in the fire," said Ms. Lentini.

2. For the rest of the morning, Jana thought about how she could help Yasmin. At the lunch table, she listed ideas on scraps of notebook paper as other kids played with their handheld game players. Jana shook her head. How could they sit there and play games at a time like this? Other kids argued about which sneakers or jeans were the best. What if you only had the clothes on your back? Finally she decided to ask the kids at her table to do something for the Ali family.

3. "Yasmin has two brothers, Luis. Do you have an extra hoodie or some jeans you could donate?" she asked the boy across from her.

Reread and use the prompts to take notes in the text.

Circle words in paragraph 2 that help you understand Jana's character. Underline the questions Jana asks herself. Write her questions here.

1. _____

2. _____

COLLABORATE

Reread paragraph 3. Talk with a partner about how Jana tries to help Yasmin and her family. Make a mark beside the text evidence that supports your discussion.

Sean Qualls

WHAT IF IT HAPPENED TO YOU?

What if a fire took all that you own?
Wouldn't you feel all alone?
What would you do?
Who would you turn to?

Please help the Ali family!
Bring extra clothes, school supplies,
and any other donations to
Ms. Lentini's class.

1. Jana's poster got everyone's attention. It made students imagine themselves in Yasmin's position. Kids donated any pocket change they had—Suni gave her whole allowance. The next day kids brought hoodies, jeans, t-shirts, and shoes. Luis donated an old game player. Trey and Ryan brought in some books and a skateboard. Soon several boxes in the classroom were full.

Reread Jana's poster. Circle the words and punctuation marks that are repeated to help you understand its purpose. Write them here:

_____

COLLABORATE

Reread the paragraph beneath Jana's poster. Talk with a partner about the impact Jana's poster had on her classmates. Underline the sentence that tells why Jana's poster made such an impact.

? **Why does the author use the same question for the selection title and Jana's poem?**

COLLABORATE

Talk About It Reread the poster on page 137. Talk with a partner about why Jana uses a series of questions instead of just asking for donations.

Cite Text Evidence What words and phrases show how the author helps you understand what Jana is trying to do? Write text evidence in the chart.

Text Evidence	Author's Purpose

Write By using the same question for the selection title and Jana's poem title, the author _____

_____

_____

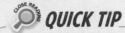
QUICK TIP

When I reread, I can use text evidence to talk about the author's purpose.

? How does Edwin Markham use figurative language to describe how the character feels and how is it similar to the way the authors use language in *Mama, I'll Give You the World* and "What If It Happened to You?"

COLLABORATE

Talk About It With a partner, read the poem. Talk about what the speaker does and how it makes him feel.

Cite Text Evidence Underline words and phrases in the poem that help you visualize how the speaker feels. Circle how you know doing something nice for someone made the speaker feel good.

Write Edwin Markham's use of figurative language is like

_____

_____

_____

_____

Comstock Images/Alamy

Two At a Fireside

I built a chimney for
a comrade old,
   I did the service not
for hope or hire—
And then I traveled on
in winter's cold,
   Yet all the day I glowed
before the fire.

— Edwin Markham

Apples to Oregon

? How does the author help you understand the characters?

COLLABORATE

Literature Anthology:
pages 384–399

Talk About It Reread page 387. Turn to your partner and talk about from which point of view the story is written.

Cite Text Evidence Which literary devices did the author use to tell you about the family? Write text evidence in the chart.

What I Learned about the Characters	Literary Devices Used by the Author

Write To help me understand the characters, the author _____

_____

_____

_____

CLOSE READING **Tip** of the **Week**

When I **reread**, I can pay attention to how the author uses point of view and other literary devices to tell me about the characters and setting. This helps me understand more about them.

©394775/Getty Images

Gabriel

? 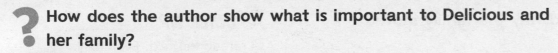How does the author show what is important to Delicious and her family?

COLLABORATE

Talk About It Reread page 391. Turn to your partner and talk about what happens when it starts to storm.

Cite Text Evidence Which details on page 391 tell you what is important to the characters in the story? Write text evidence in the chart.

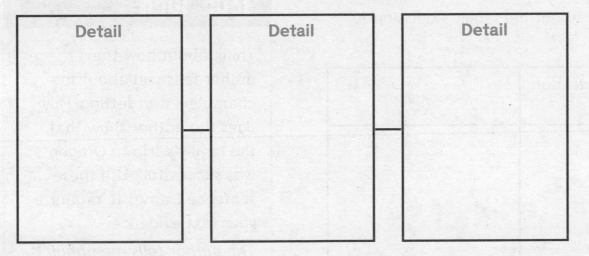

Detail	Detail	Detail

Write The author shows what is important to Delicious and her family _____

_____

_____

QUICK TIP

I can use these sentence frames when we talk about Delicious and her family.

When it starts to storm, the author describes . . .

This helps me understand . . .

? **How does the illustration help you understand why the family moved to Oregon?**

COLLABORATE

Talk About It Reread page 398 and look at the illustration on page 399. Turn to your partner and talk about what happens to the family when they get to Oregon.

Cite Text Evidence Compare the end of the story with what is shown in the illustration. What conclusions can you draw about the family's decision to move to Oregon?

What the Text Says	What the Illustration Shows	Conclusions

Write The illustration helps me to understand that the family moved to

Oregon to _____

_____

QUICK TIP

As I reread the text, I will think about how the illustration helps me understand why the family moved west.

Your Turn

Think about how the author tells you about the characters and setting. How does the author show that the family's trip to Oregon was successful? Use these sentence frames to organize your text evidence.

The author tells me about Delicious and her family by using . . .

Through descriptive details, I learned . . .

The illustrations help me understand . . .

Go Digital!
Write your response online.

Westward Bound: Settling the American West

The Reasons Why

[1]   Many Americans were more than willing to pack up and head west. The east coast was crowded due to the arrival of immigrants from Europe. Work was hard to find and did not pay well. Many people had factory jobs. This type of work involved long hours and little money. Large families were forced to live together in small spaces. People believed the West offered an opportunity for a better life. Many liked the idea of owning land and becoming farmers.

[2]   People also moved west for freedom. Slavery was still practiced in the United States during this time. Many escaped slaves headed west, where they had a chance to be free. Other groups of people migrated west so that they could practice their religion freely. For example, large groups of Mormons traveled to Utah for this reason.

Reread and use the prompts to take notes in the text.

Reread paragraph 1. Number the reasons why people were willing to move west. Write two examples here.

1. _____

2. _____

COLLABORATE

Reread paragraph 2. Talk with a partner about how freedom was another important reason why people moved west.

Why is "The Reasons Why" a good heading for this section? Use your annotations to support your response.

_____

_____

_____

The Challenges Ahead

1   Weather was always an important consideration for pioneers. Thunderstorms, snow, wind, and drought were all concerns. The dry heat of the desert and lack of water posed real dangers, especially in the Southwest. Pioneers traveling Northwest faced cold and snowy mountain passes.

2   There were other hardships on the trail, too. Pioneers dealt with illness, hunger, exhaustion, and natural dangers, such as snake bites. People had to work together to ensure that they survived. They formed long wagon trains and traveled the trails in large groups. Still, in other parts of the trails, cool rivers and lakes welcomed them, and open prairies provided the food they needed. Some Native Americans showed great kindness to the pioneers and helped them along their way.

Reread paragraph 1. Circle the words the author uses to help you understand the challenges faced by pioneers on the trail.

Why is "The Challenges Ahead" a good heading for this section? Use your annotations to support your response.

_____

_____

_____

COLLABORATE

Reread paragraph 2. Talk about how pioneers dealt with the hardships they faced. Underline two ways the pioneers were able to overcome these challenges.

? How does the author organize the information to help you understand the westward migration?

Talk About It Reread the headings on pages 143 and 144. Talk with a partner about why the information is broken up into two different sections.

Cite Text Evidence How does the author organize the information in the two sections? Write text evidence in the chart.

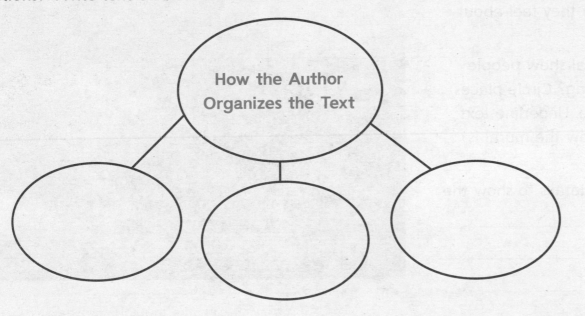

How the Author Organizes the Text

Write To help me understand the westward migration, the author organizes the information _____

_____

_____

_____

When I reread, I can look at how the text is organized by the author. This helps me understand the information on the topic.

? How does the artist's use of details in the mural compare with the way the authors used words and phrases to describe the journey west across America in *Apples to Oregon* and "Westward Bound: Settling the American West"?

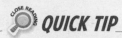

COLLABORATE

Talk About It Look at the mural and read the caption. Talk with a partner about what you see. Choose some of the people in it and discuss how you know how they feel about their journey.

Cite Text Evidence What clues in the mural show people who feel hopeful about where they are going? Circle places in the mural that show challenges they face. Underline text in the caption that helps you understand how the mural is important to America's history.

Write The way the artist and authors use details to show the journey westward helps me _____

_____

_____

_____

_____

Architect of the Capitol

This mural hangs in the United States Capitol Building in Washington, D.C. It was painted in 1862 by a German artist named Emanual Leutze. The painting's title is a verse from a poem about art and learning in America. It is called *Westward the Course of the Empire Takes Its Way*.

Literature Anthology: pages 406–421

Reread

How Ben Franklin Stole the Lightning

 How does the author's introduction of Ben Franklin help you understand the impact he had?

Talk About It Reread page 409. Turn to your partner and talk about some of Ben Franklin's accomplishments.

Cite Text Evidence What words and punctuation help you understand Ben Franklin's influence? Write text evidence in the chart.

Author's Words and Punctuation	Conclusions about Ben Franklin

Write The author's introduction of Ben Franklin helps me understand his impact by _____

_____

_____

_____

Tip of the Week

When I **reread**, I can think about how the author presents information. I look for text evidence to answer questions.

Brady

? Why is the author's description of Ben Franklin's constant experimentation an important part of the biography?

COLLABORATE

Talk About It Reread paragraphs 3–6 on page 415. Turn to your partner and talk about what made Ben Franklin's experiments with electricity different.

Cite Text Evidence What does the author want you to understand about Ben Franklin that made him different from everyone else who was experimenting with electricity at the time? Write text evidence in the web.

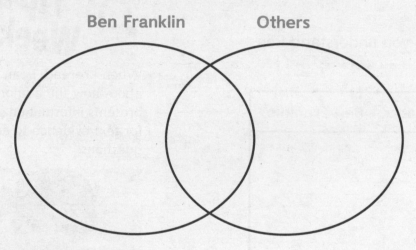

Ben Franklin   Others

Write The way the author describes Ben Franklin's experimentation is

important because _____

_____

_____

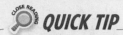
Ben Franklin invented many things, including the adage, or saying, "an apple a day keeps the doctor away." Sometimes when you are reading, you may come across other adages like this one. Stop and think about what they mean. Write them in your Writer's Notebook.

? How does the author help you understand that Ben Franklin's invention of the lightning rod is important?

Talk About It Reread pages 418 and 419. Turn to your partner and talk about how the author describes Ben's invention of the lightning rod.

Cite Text Evidence What words and phrases help you understand the importance of the invention of the lightning rod? Write text evidence.

What the Author Says	What This Means

Write The author thinks that Ben Franklin's invention of the lightning rod was

important because _____

_____

QUICK TIP

When I reread, I can think about what the author says about Ben Franklin's invention. This will help me understand its importance.

Your Turn

Think about how Rosalyn Schanzer talks about Ben Franklin's accomplishments. How does she help you understand that Ben Franklin was a great problem-solver? Use these sentence frames to organize your text evidence.

Rosalyn Schanzer introduces Ben Franklin by . . .

Then she describes how . . .
Finally, she shows that . . .

Go Digital!
Write your response online.

Energy Is Everywhere!

Kinds of Energy

1   Scientists define energy as the ability to apply force. So, energy is used when someone or something flies, falls, runs, beeps, moves, or cooks. But energy is not always that obvious because there are many different kinds. Chemical energy is stored in things such as petroleum, coal, wood—even food. Mechanical energy is stored in objects under tension such as springs on trampolines. Mechanical energy may also be energy in motion, such as the energy of wind blowing down branches during a storm.

2   The sun is a source of light energy. Sunlight makes life possible. Plants transform the sun's light energy into chemical energy, or food. You can think about it this way—when you eat oatmeal for breakfast and then run to the bus stop, your motion energy is a result of sunlight helping oat plants to grow.

Reread and use the prompts to take notes in the text.

Underline the definition of energy the author gives in paragraph 1. Then circle the two kinds of energy mentioned in the paragraph.

COLLABORATE

Talk with a partner about how the author explains light energy in paragraph 2. In your own words, write how sunlight makes life possible.

_____

_____

Electrical Energy

1 Electrical energy is an energy carrier. That means it is created from certain forms of energy and can then produce other forms of energy. For example, when you dry your hair after a shower, you plug in a hair dryer and turn it on. That may seem simple, but many things happen before your hair dries. First, the electricity for the hair dryer comes from a power plant, which is the energy source. This energy source transforms the chemical energy of oil, coal, or natural gas into electric charges. These electric charges, or electricity, then follow wires to the socket and into your hair dryer, creating a current. So when you flip a switch to turn the hair dryer on, that action provides a path for the electrical current. It also transforms electrical energy into thermal and mechanical energy—the heat and blowing air.

Reread the excerpt. Underline the words the author uses to define electrical energy.

COLLABORATE

Reread the example of how electrical energy is used when you turn on a hair dryer. Talk with a partner about the steps that take place. Number each step in the margin.

How does the author help you understand electrical energy? Use your annotations to support your response.

_____

_____

_____

Why does the author think it is important to learn about energy?

 **QUICK TIP**

When I reread, I can make an inference about why the author thinks the topic is important.

COLLABORATE

Talk About It Reread the excerpts on pages 150 and 151. With a partner, compare the texts and talk about what the author wants you to know about energy.

Cite Text Evidence What words help you understand what the author thinks about energy? Write text evidence in the web.

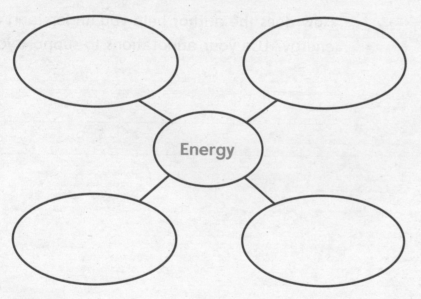

Energy

Write The author thinks that it is important to learn about energy _____

_____

_____

? How do the song lyrics and the words and phrases used by the authors of *How Ben Franklin Stole the Lightning* and "Energy is Everywhere!" help you understand what inventors are like?

COLLABORATE

Talk About It Read the lyrics. Talk with a partner about how the songwriter organizes the information and how it shows what he thinks about inventors.

Cite Text Evidence Circle the words and phrases in the lyrics that describe inventors. Underline how the inventors make the world a better place to live.

Write The songwriter and authors help me understand that

_____

_____

_____

_____

Ingram Publishing/Alamy

QUICK TIP
CLOSE READING

I can use the words and phrases in the lyrics that describe inventors. This will help me compare the song to texts.

from **Inventor Song**

Oh it took Bell to make the telephone ring,
And it took Edison to light up our way.
It took Robert Fulton in a steamboat,
To go chug-chug-chugging down
the bay.

Otis made the elevator go up,
McCormick's reaper reaped
the rye.
So when you're spelling
the word, America,
Don't forget to dot the I....
for the inventors, don't
forget to dot the I!

A Drop of Water

 How does the author use photographs to help explain complex ideas?

COLLABORATE

Talk About It Reread page 430. Then analyze the photographs on page 431. Turn to your partner and describe what is happening.

Cite Text Evidence How do the photographs and text go together? Write text evidence in the chart below.

What the Text Says	→	What the Photos Show
	→	
	→	
	→	
	→	

Write The photos support the text because _____

_____

_____

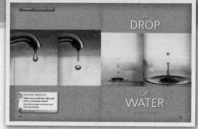

Literature Anthology:
pages 428–445

CLOSE READING
Tip of the Week

When I **reread**, I can look at how the author uses photographs to help me understand the text. I look for text evidence to answer questions.

Delia

Jose Luis Pelaez Inc/Blend Images/Getty Images Plus/Getty Images

? How does the author use a blue drop of water to explain how water becomes ice?

COLLABORATE

Talk About It Reread the first paragraph on page 432. Turn to your partner and talk about what happens to the blue drop when it becomes ice.

Cite Text Evidence How does the author help you understand the difference between the molecules in liquid water and ice? Write text evidence in the diagram.

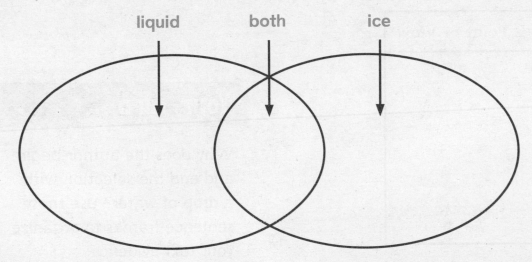

liquid   both   ice

Write The author uses a blue drop of water to explain how water becomes ice

because _____

_____

_____

I can use these sentence frames when we talk about how ice forms.

The author uses the blue drop of water to . . .

This helps me understand . . .

? **How does the author help you understand how he feels about water?**

COLLABORATE

Talk About It Reread the last paragraph on page 445. Turn to your partner and discuss why the author says that water is precious.

Cite Text Evidence What reasons does the author provide to help you understand his point of view about water? Write text evidence in the chart below.

Text Evidence	Author's Point of View

Write The author helps me understand how he feels about water _____

_____

_____

_____

 **QUICK TIP**

To find the author's point of view, I look for details such as reasons and evidence, that tell me how he feels.

Your Turn

Why does the author begin and end the selection with a drop of water? Use these sentence frames to organize your text evidence.

The author begins the selection . . .

I read that the drop of water . . .

At the end of the selection . . .

Go Digital!
Write your response online.

The Incredible Shrinking Potion

Richard Johnson

1   It began as a simple science project.

2   It was only one week ago that Isabel, Mariela, and Hector were working on a shrinking potion that would amaze everyone at the science fair. Mariela and Isabel had perfected the potion, but it was Hector who had created the antidote. Since his discovery, Hector had become less interested in winning the science fair prize and more interested in how this experiment could increase his popularity. His short stature made him practically invisible to everyone at Washington Elementary School.

3   That wasn't the case anymore—now the entire class was looking up at Hector. He had come to the science lab bearing "special" cupcakes, which made it easy for him to shrink the entire class, including his science teacher, Ms. Sampson. Hector smirked as he placed his miniature classmates inside the tank of Rambo, the class pet.

Reread and use the prompts to take notes in the text.

How does the author help you understand the reason why Hector shrinks his classmates? Underline two sentences that explain Hector's motivation. Write them here.

_____

_____

_____

_____

_____

COLLABORATE

Talk with a partner about what kind of character Hector is. Circle words the author uses to describe Hector and his actions.

4   Isabel and Mariela overheard the shrinking shrieks of their classmates outside the classroom door. The girls had been late to lab again. Upon peering inside, they quickly realized they had to do something. Mariela saw that Rambo, outfitted with a vest of tiny tubes, was sniffing merrily outside his tank.

5   "Rambo has the antidote!" Mariela whispered to Isabel. "We will have to shrink ourselves to sneak inside and get the antidote. Then we can help everyone out of the tank!" With shaking hands, Isabel pulled out a vial. The girls took a deep breath and sipped the shrinking potion. The world around them began to grow . . . .

6   As Isabel and Mariela walked under the classroom door, everything was magnified to the extreme. Desks and chairs towered over them—even the complex details of each nut and screw became clear, as if viewed under a microscope. The girls made their way to the other side of the lab, dodging mountainous cupcake crumbs and wads of gooey gum.

Reread paragraphs 4 and 5. Draw a box around the words the author uses to describe what Isabel and Mariela see and hear outside of their classroom door.

COLLABORATE

Reread paragraph 6. Talk about what the girls see when they walk under the classroom door.

Circle words the author uses to describe what Isabel and Mariela see. Write them here.

_____

? How does the author use words and phrases to help you visualize what the classroom looks like to Isabel and Mariela?

Talk About It Reread excerpt on page 158. Talk with a partner about why Mariela and Isabela take the shrinking potion.

Cite Text Evidence What words does the author use to describe the classroom from Isabel and Mariela's point of view? Write text evidence in the chart.

Text Evidence	What I Visualize

Write The author uses words and phrases to helps me visualize what Isabel and Mariela see by _____

_____

_____

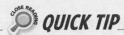

QUICK TIP

When I reread, I look at the way the author describes the characters and setting to picture what is happening in the story.

COLLABORATE

? How do the photographer and the authors of *A Drop of Water* and "The Incredible Shrinking Potion" help you understand what you can discover when you look at things closely?

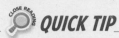
Talk About It Read the caption and look at the series of photographs. Talk with a partner about how the photographer broke the horse's motions into smaller parts.

Cite Text Evidence Circle a clue in each photograph that changes from one frame to the next.

Write Eadweard Muybridge's photographs are like _____

_____

_____

_____

Courtesy National Gallery of Art, Washington

Eadweard Muybridge was a famous photographer who took pictures of many animals and people in motion. This series of photographs is called "Animal Locomotion, Plate 626" and it was created in 1887.

Rediscovering Our Spanish Beginnings

Literature Anthology: pages 452–455

? How does the author use text features to help you understand our Spanish beginnings?

COLLABORATE

Talk About It Reread page 453. Turn to your partner and talk about how St. Augustine was founded.

Cite Text Evidence What clues from the text features help you understand the topic better? Write evidence in the chart and explain how it helps.

Illustrations and Captions	Heading	How They Help

Write The author's use of text features helps me to _____.

_____

_____

_____

CLOSE READING
Tip of the **Week**

I can use text features to help me understand the topic. I look for text evidence to answer questions.

Byron

KidStock/Blend Images/Getty Images

How does the author use sidebars to connect the past and present?

COLLABORATE

Talk About It Reread pages 454 and 455. Turn to your partner and talk about how the information provided in the sidebars supports the main text.

Cite Text Evidence What information from the sidebars add to your understanding of the past and present Spanish influence? Write it in the web.

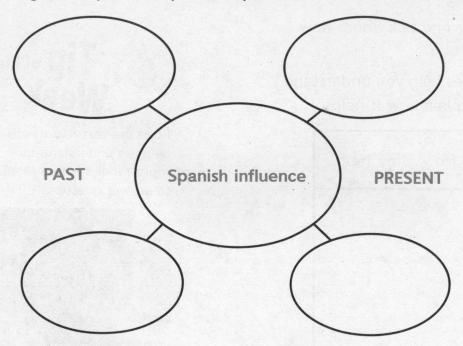

PAST   Spanish influence   PRESENT

Write The author uses sidebars to help me understand the connection

between the past and present by _____

_____

_____

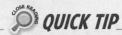 **QUICK TIP**

When I reread, I can use the sidebar to help me understand more about the topic.

Your Turn

How does the author's use of text features help you understand how history has shaped America's culture? Use these sentence frames to organize text evidence.

The author uses text features to . . .

This helps me understand . . .

Go Digital!
Write your response online.

History's Mysteries

Finding Popham

1 In 1607, a crew of 125 English colonists set out on an expedition. They landed on Maine's coast. They erected a small settlement and named it for its principal backer, Sir John Popham, and his nephew George. But the Popham Colony—England's first attempt at a New England settlement—didn't survive. One year later, the colonists boarded their ship and sailed home.

2 For centuries, no one knew precisely where the colony had been. Then archaeologist Jeffrey Brain began excavating the area in 1994. After ten years of digging, Brain and his team uncovered traces of the colony's storehouse, a hearth (or floor of a fireplace), and stoneware fragments. Their work helped unearth clues about the way the colony lived.

Reread and use the prompts to take notes in the text.

Make a mark in the margin beside the events in paragraph 1 that tell what the English colonists did in 1607.

Underline what happened to the colonists one year later.

COLLABORATE

Reread paragraph 2. Talk with a partner about what Jeffrey Brain found. Circle text evidence to support your discussion.

Draw a box around the dates and time order words used by the author to highlight the importance of Brain's discovery. Write them here.

_____

_____

? **How do you know how the author feels about archaeology?**

COLLABORATE

Talk About It Reread the excerpt on page 163. Talk with a partner about why the author might put so much emphasis on dates and time order words in the selection.

Cite Text Evidence In what ways does the author's word choice help you understand how he feels about archaeology? Write text evidence in the chart.

Text Evidence	Author's Point of View

Write I know how the author feels about archaeology because _____

_____

_____

CLOSE READING

QUICK TIP

When I reread, I can look at words and phrases to help me understand how the author feels.

Integrate

? How do you know that learning about the history of the Serpent Mound, St. Augustine, and the Popham colony will help you understand the present?

COLLABORATE

Talk About It Look at the photograph and read the caption. Talk with a partner about what the photograph of the Serpent Mound shows.

Cite Text Evidence With a pencil, trace around the snake. Underline clues in the caption that describe why the mound is important. Think about how the photographer and authors of "Rediscovering Our Spanish Beginnings" and "History's Mysteries" help you understand how the past helps archaeologists understand the present.

Write The photographer and authors help me understand that the past helps explain the present by

_____

_____

_____

_____

©Richard A. Ccoke/Corbis

> **QUICK TIP**
> I can think about what the archaeologists learned in this week's selections. This will help me compare them to the photograph of the Serpent Mound.

The Serpent Mound is a mound of dirt in the shape of a long snake in Ohio. It was declared a National Historic Landmark. Researchers and archaeologists believe the mound was built by an ancient culture. This photograph shows an aerial view of the 1,345-foot-long serpent.

The Game of Silence

? Why does the author want you to understand how frustrating and challenging the game of silence is?

Literature Anthology: pages 458–469

COLLABORATE

Talk About It Reread page 462. Turn to your partner and talk about why Omakayas struggles to stay quiet during the game.

Cite Text Evidence What details show how challenging the game is for Omakayas? Write text evidence in the chart.

Sensory Details	Why is this effective?

Write The author wants me to understand how frustrating and challenging the game is because _____

_____

Tip of the Week

CLOSE READING

When I **reread**, I can think about how the author uses sensory details to help me understand why the characters are playing the game. I look for text evidence to answer questions.

Elena

JUPITERIMAGES/Polka Dot/Alamy

? **How does the author use words and phrases to create a sense of community?**

COLLABORATE

Talk About It Reread page 465. Turn to your partner and talk about how the author describes the lodge and the meal.

Cite Text Evidence What sensory details does the author use to describe the lodge and the meal? Write text evidence in the web below.

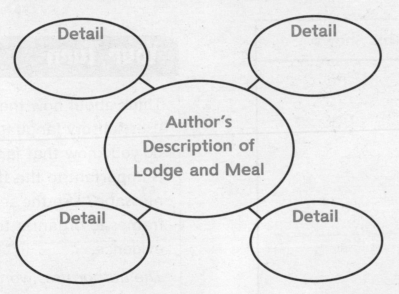

Detail

Detail

Author's Description of Lodge and Meal

Detail

Detail

Write The author uses words and phrases to create a sense of community by

_____

_____

_____

QUICK TIP

I can use these sentence frames when we talk about community.
The author describes the lodge and meal . . .

This helps me visualize . . .

How does the author show that the Ojibwe valued the children in their tribe?

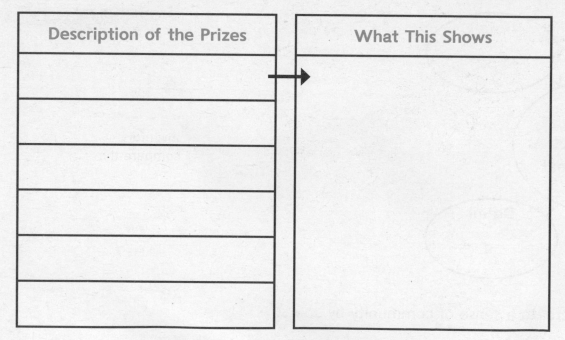

COLLABORATE

Talk About It Reread pages 466–467. Turn to your partner and talk about how the children knew that the meeting was an important one.

Cite Text Evidence How does the author's description of the prizes help you understand what is important to the Ojibwe tribe? Write text evidence below.

Description of the Prizes	What This Shows

Write The author shows that the Ojibwe valued the children in their tribe by

_____

_____

 **QUICK TIP**

When I reread the author's description of the prizes, I can analyze the way the children respond to them. This helps me understand their role in the tribe.

Your Turn

Think about how the author uses sensory language. How do you know that family is important to the story's message? Use the sentence frames to organize text evidence.

The author uses words and phrases to help me visualize . . .

This is important to the story's message because . . .

It helps me understand . . .

Go Digital!
Write your response online.

Native Americans: Yesterday and Today

Native Americans of Long Ago

[1]   Yet those ways of life changed once Europeans arrived. Scholars believe thousands, perhaps millions, of Native Americans died from diseases brought by white settlers in the 1700s. As the United States expanded, wars between the settlers and tribes erupted. Of the Native Americans who survived, many retreated from their lands. The rest were forced westward by white settlers and soldiers. The Indian Removal Act of 1830 relocated tribes west of the Mississippi River. This opened up 25 million acres to settlement. Native American groups in all regions had to cope with loss. While adapting to new environments, tribes struggled to maintain traditions.

Reread and use the prompts to take notes in the text.

Circle strong words the author uses to describe what happened between white settlers and soldiers and the Native Americans. Write three of those words here.

1. _____

2. _____

3. _____

COLLABORATE

Talk with a partner about how life changed for the Native Americans after the Europeans arrived. What does the author's description help you understand about life for Native Americans of long ago?

_____

_____

_____

Native Americans Today

1   These days, Native people lead different lives from their ancestors. Some groups living on reservations face poverty; others have thrived economically. The wild rice that we buy today comes largely from the Ojibwe reservation. Coal mining and tourism have supported the Hopi people. The Cherokee of Oklahoma have built hotels, hospitals, and entertainment centers. Tourism is an important source of income for the Seminole.

2   Despite what they have endured, Native Americans today maintain ways to honor their culture and history. Dances and gatherings called powwows allow them to celebrate ancient traditions. Sharing stories with each new generation also helps to keep the Native American past alive in the present.

Reread paragraph 1. Underline the sentence that compares Native Americans of long ago with Native people today. Circle the tribes mentioned that are thriving economically.

COLLABORATE

Reread paragraph 2. Talk about how Native Americans today honor their cultural traditions. Make a mark in the margin beside each clue. Write those two ways here.

1. _____

2. _____

How does the author organize the text to show how life changed for Native Americans?

Talk About It Reread the two excerpts on pages 169 and 170. With a partner, talk about what you learn about Native Americans under each heading.

Cite Text Evidence Draw a box around the headings for each excerpt. Why are these headings appropriate? Write text evidence in the chart.

"Native Americans of Long Ago"	"Native Americans Today"

Write The author organizes the text to show how life changed for Native Americans by _____

_____

_____

QUICK TIP

When I reread, I look closely at the headings. Headings often tell the most important idea of a section of text.

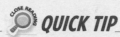

? How does the photographer express a similar point of view about traditions as the authors of *The Game of Silence* and "Native Americans: Yesterday and Today"?

COLLABORATE

Talk About It Look at the photograph and read the caption. Talk with a partner about how the photographer shows that traditions are important.

Cite Text Evidence Circle clues in the photograph that show both traditions and family. Underline a phrase in the caption that tells more about how the photograph shows tradition. Think about the selections you read this week and how the authors use words and phrases to tell their point of view.

Write The photographer's point of view is like

_____

_____

_____

_____

Coral Coolahan/Getty Images

A Navajo woman teaches her granddaughter the skill of hand spinning.

Valley of the Moon

? **Why does the author compare Miguela and María Rosalia's reactions to the diary?**

Literature Anthology: pages 476–489

Talk About It Reread the diary entry on page 478. Turn to a partner and talk about how Miguela and María Rosalia feel about reading and writing.

Cite Text Evidence What does the author's comparison tell you about the characters? Write text evidence in the diagram.

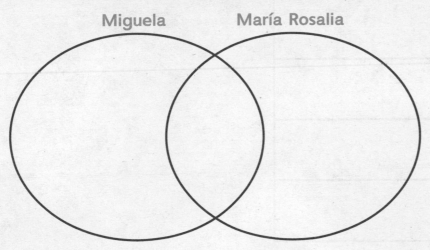

Miguela   María Rosalia

Write The author compares Miguela and María Rosalia to _____

_____

Tip of the **Week**

When I **reread**, I think about how the author compares two characters. I look for text evidence to answer questions.

Zach

? **Why is the author's choice to write the story as a series of diary entries effective?**

COLLABORATE

Talk About It Reread page 480. Turn to your partner and talk about what you learn about María Rosalia from her diary entry.

Cite Text Evidence What words and phrases help you understand María Rosalia's character? Write text evidence in the chart and tell why it is effective.

What María Rosalia Writes	Why This Is Effective

Write The author's choice to write the story as a series of diary entries is

effective because _____

_____

_____

QUICK TIP

I can use these sentence frames when we talk about the diary entries.

The author uses diary entries to . . .

This helps me understand that María Rosalia is . . .

? **How does the author use figurative language to help you visualize how María Rosalia feels about writing?**

 **QUICK TIP**

When I reread, I look at the author's word choice to help me understand how María Rosalia feels.

COLLABORATE

Talk About It Reread the first diary entry on page 484. Turn to your partner and talk about how and when María Rosalia is able to write.

Cite Text Evidence What does the author's word choice tell you about María Rosalia's feelings about writing? Write text evidence in the chart.

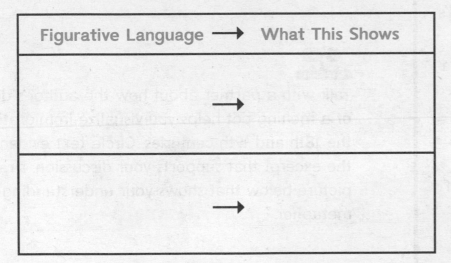

Figurative Language ➝	What This Shows
➝	
➝	

Write The author's use of figurative language shows how María Rosalia feels

about writing by _____

_____

_____

Your Turn

How does the author use María Rosalia's diary entries to help you learn about her character and what's important to her? Use these sentence frames to organize your text evidence.

The author uses María Rosalia's diary entries to . . .

She uses words and phrases to help me visualize . . .

This helps me understand . . .

Go Digital!
Write your response online.

One Nation, Many Cultures

A Land of Opportunity

1   In the 18th and 19th centuries, the term "melting pot" was a popular metaphor used to describe how immigrants assimilated into our culture—that is, they left behind their homeland's customs to forge a new American identity.

2   Immigrants viewed moving to our nation as a chance for a better life. Many Europeans endured hardships in their home countries. They dealt with poverty and hunger. They did not have jobs. Many were unable to feed their families. The United States, however, was brimming with opportunities. Unskilled laborers could work in factories. Finally they could earn enough to provide for their families. Some immigrants longed to move west and own land. Others wanted to work on the railroad.

Reread and use the prompts to take notes in the text.

Underline the reasons in paragraph 2 that tell why immigrants came to America. In your own words, summarize what immigrants hoped for.

_____

_____

COLLABORATE

Talk with a partner about how the author's description of a melting pot helps you visualize immigration in the 18th and 19th centuries. Circle text evidence in the excerpt that supports your discussion. Draw a picture below that shows your understanding of their metaphor.

Immigration Today

1   A more recent theory on American culture—the stew pot theory—is a combination of the melting pot and salad bowl theories. It compares immigrants to ingredients that take on other flavors and tastes as new ingredients are added to the pot. In other words, immigrants take on American characteristics to blend in and show obedience to national laws, but they also hold onto their cultural backgrounds. This adds to the diversity of the country.

2   Today, immigrants still arrive from all over the world. The majority of them come from Latin America. These immigrants come here for the same reasons that immigrants came here hundreds of years ago. They come for freedom and a chance at a better life. They might be escaping poverty or war in their homelands. Some immigrants come to the United States to work and send money back to their families.

Reread paragraph 1. Underline the author's description of the stew pot theory. How is the stew pot theory different from the melting pot theory in the first excerpt? Use annotations to support your response.

_____

_____

_____

_____

COLLABORATE

Reread paragraph 2. Talk about why immigrants still come to America. What is the author's purpose in providing the reasons why immigrants still come to America today? Use text evidence in your response.

_____

_____

_____

How does the author help you understand the role of immigration in American culture?

Talk About It Reread the two excerpts on pages 176 and 177. Talk with a partner about what you notice about why immigrants came to America.

Cite Text Evidence What reasons does the author repeat in both excerpts? Write text evidence in the diagram and then compare and contrast the first immigrants to immigrants today.

First Immigrants   Immigrants Today

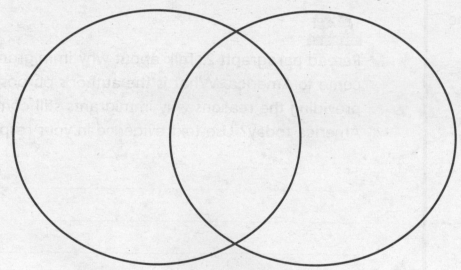

Write The author helps you understand the role of immigration in American culture by _____

_____

QUICK TIP

I see images that tell a story of long ago. This will help me compare it to María Rosalia's diary in *Valley of the Moon*.

? How do you know that the cave painting in the photograph and María Rosalia's diary are important records of the past?

COLLABORATE

Talk About It Look at the cave painting and read the caption. Talk about what it can help people today learn about Native Americans.

Cite Text Evidence Circle clues in the cave painting that tell about how the Native Americans lived. Reread the caption. Underline how you know these petroglyphs are important today.

Write I know that both the cave paintings and María

Rosalia's diary are important records because _____

_____

_____

_____

©DLILLC/Corbis

Newspaper Rock State Historic Monument in Utah has one of the largest known collections of petroglyphs like this one. Petroglyphs are cave paintings created by Native Americans many years ago. At the site, there is more than 650 rock art designs.

Energy Island

? **Why does the author emphasize the word *ordinary* when describing the island of Samsø?**

Literature Anthology: pages 496–513

Talk About It Reread page 498. Turn to your partner and discuss what the author tells you about the island of Samsø.

Cite Text Evidence What does the author describe as ordinary? Write text evidence in the web below.

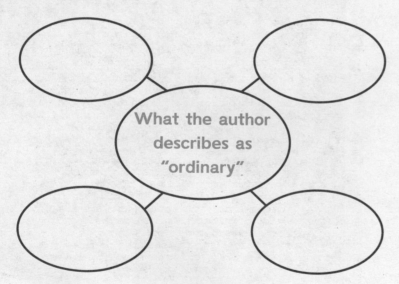

What the author describes as "ordinary"

Tip of the Week

When I **reread**, I think about how the author uses word choice. I look for text evidence to answer questions.

Kisha

Write The author emphasizes the word *ordinary* when describing the island of Samsø to _____

_____

_____

Kali Nine LLC/iStock/360/Getty Images

How is the author's use of the phrase "hold on to your hats" important to the idea for Samsø's energy independence?

Talk About It Reread page 501. Turn to your partner and talk about the idea Kathrine suggests for the island. Based on her suggestion, why would the residents of Samsø need to hold on to their hats?

Cite Text Evidence Explain the two meanings of "hold on to your hats" as it relates to the story. Write text evidence in the chart below.

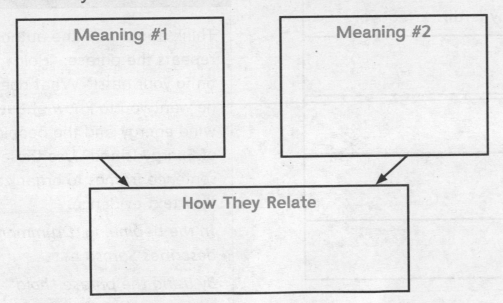

Meaning #1

Meaning #2

How They Relate

QUICK TIP

I can use these sentence frames when we talk about Kathrine's idea.

Kathrine suggests using wind energy because . . .

The residents should hold on to their hats because . . .

Write The author's use of the phrase "hold on to your hats" is important to the idea for Samsø's energy independence because _____

_____

_____

? **Why does the author want you to picture an active, enthusiastic island at the end of the selection?**

COLLABORATE

Talk About It Reread page 510. Turn to your partner and discuss how the island of Samsø has changed.

Cite Text Evidence How does the author's word choice show enthusiasm for the changes on the island? Write text evidence in the chart below.

Description of Samsø	Why is this effective?

Write The author wants you to picture an active, enthusiastic island at the end of the selection to _____

_____

_____

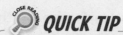

QUICK TIP

When I reread, I can think about why the author chooses certain words and phrases. This helps me understand the author's purpose.

Your Turn

Think about how the author repeats the phrase, "Hold on to your hats!" What does he want you to know about wind energy and the people of Energy Island? Use these sentence frames to organize your text evidence.

In the beginning, Drummond describes Samsø as . . .

By using the phrase "hold on to your hats," the author shows . . .

At the end of the selection, the author points out how . . .

Go Digital!
Write your response online.

Of Fire and Water

The Gift of Fire

1   To appease the angry Zeus, humans offered him abundant sacrifices. They kept little for themselves.

2   Prometheus thought this was wrong. He tricked Zeus into choosing a cleverly disguised sacrificial dish rather than a richer dish for his offering. The dish Zeus chose looked delicious on the outside, but within it consisted entirely of fat and bones. When Zeus realized the trick, he took fire away from humans.

3   Prometheus pleaded with Zeus to change his mind, but Zeus forbade him to bring fire to humans. Prometheus watched his creations eat raw meat and shiver in the cold and dark. Finally, he went to Athena for help, and she led Prometheus to a hidden entrance to Mount Olympus where he could capture fire for humans.

Reread and use the prompts to take notes in the text.

Underline two examples the author gives to show what happened to humans when fire was taken from them. Write your examples here.

1. _____

2. _____

Talk with a partner about how the author shows the importance of fire. Circle text evidence that shows one of the gods felt the need to do something. How does the title fit the myth's message?

Use your annotations to support your response.

_____

_____

Water vs. Wisdom

1   Poseidon was the first to offer a gift. Raising his trident high over his head, he struck the rocky hill with a powerful blow. Cecrops watched in amazement as the hole filled with water. In the hot, dry land of Greece, water was a precious resource.

2   The people of Attica were impressed. They seemed ready to rule in favor of Poseidon until Athena told Cecrops to taste the water. A servant brought a cup to the king, who drank it and spit it out. It was salt water! There was no use for that in Attica.

3   Then, Athena came forward with the branch of a tree that no human had seen before. She planted the branch in the ground, and an olive tree sprang up in its place. The king nodded, pleased. His people now had a source of food, wood, and oil.

Reread paragraph 1. Circle the words the author uses to emphasize the importance of water to the people of Attica. Write those words here:

_____

COLLABORATE

Reread paragraphs 2 and 3. Talk about how the author compares Poseidon's and Athena's gifts to the people of Attica. If water was such an important resource to the people of Attica, why do they choose Athena's gift?

Why is "Water vs. Wisdom" a good title for this myth? Use your annotations to support your response.

_____

_____

_____

What does the author suggest about resources in both myths?

QUICK TIP
When I reread, I think about what the texts have in common. This helps me determine the author's message.

COLLABORATE

Talk About It Reread the paragraphs on pages 183 and 184. With a partner, compare the information in these myths. What does the author want you to understand about resources?

Cite Text Evidence Compare and contrast what the myths suggest about resources. Write text evidence in the diagram below.

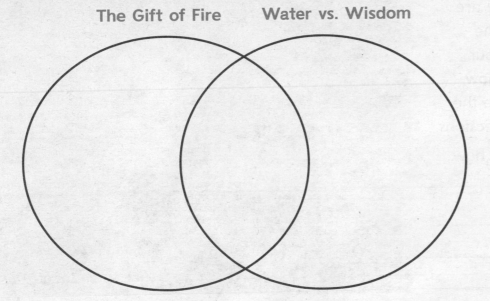

The Gift of Fire   Water vs. Wisdom

Write The author suggests that resources _____

_____

_____

? **How does the artist focus your attention on the resources in the painting in the same way that the authors of *Energy Island* and "Of Fire and Water" help you understand the importance of natural resources?**

COLLABORATE

Talk About It With a partner, look at the painting and read the caption. Talk about the natural resources you see and how some of them are being used.

Cite Text Evidence Circle clues in the painting and caption that show natural resources and how they are being used. Draw a line to separate the sky and the water. The artist composed the painting so that your eye would notice the windmill. Then think about how the authors use words and phrases to help you see the importance of natural resources in this week's selections.

Write The artist and authors help me understand how important natural resources are by _____

_____

_____

_____

_____

Rijksmuseum, Amsterdam

This oil painting is called *The Windmill at Wijk bij Duurstede*. It was painted by Dutch artist, Jacob van Ruisdael, between 1668 and 1670.

The Big Picture of Economics

Literature Anthology:
pages 520–529

? How does the author use photos and illustrations to help you understand how our economy has changed over time?

COLLABORATE

Talk About It Reread page 522 and then look at the illustration and photo. Talk with a partner about how the illustration and photo support the text.

Cite Text Evidence How does the author show what our economy was like long ago? Use the text and text features to write evidence in the chart below.

CLOSE READING

Tip of the Week

When I **reread**, I look closely at the text features the author uses to support the text. This helps me understand how our economy has changed over time.

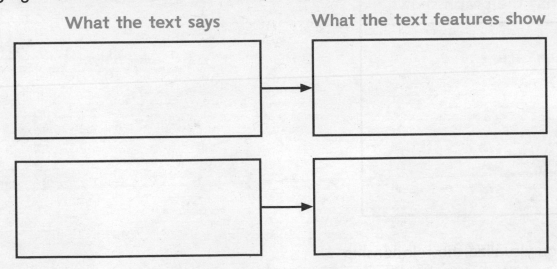

What the text says	What the text features show

Hassan

Write The author's use of photos and illustrations help me understand how our economy has changed by _____

_____

_____

azgAr Donmaz/E+/Getty Images

? How does the author use text features to help you visualize the relationship between supply and demand in a free market?

COLLABORATE

Talk About It Reread page 527. Look at the illustration on page 526 and the graph on page 527. Turn to your partner and talk about who is selling the most lemonade and who is selling the least.

Cite Text Evidence How do the illustration and graph support the author's explanation of supply and demand? Write text evidence in the chart below.

What the illustration shows	What the graph shows

Write The author's use of text features help you visualize the relationship

between supply and demand in a free market by _____

_____

_____

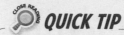
QUICK TIP

I can use these sentence frames when I talk about the lemonade sales.

The booth that sells the most lemonade is . . .

The booth that sells the least lemonade is . . .

? **How does the author help you understand how people get their products today?**

Talk About It Reread paragraphs 1 and 2 on page 528. Look at the illustration. Turn to your partner and talk about what a global marketplace is.

Cite Text Evidence How does the illustration support the author's explanation of a global marketplace? Write text evidence in the chart below.

What the text says	What the illustration shows

Write The author helps you understand how people get their products today

by _____

_____

_____

QUICK TIP

I can look at the illustration to understand what the author means by global marketplace. This will help me visualize how people get products today.

Your Turn

How do the text features help you understand how the role of money has changed over time? Use these sentence frames to organize your text evidence.

The author uses illustration and captions to help me understand that . . .

He also uses text features to show . . .

This helps me see how the role of money has changed because . . .

Go Digital!
Write your response online.

The Miller's Good Luck

1.   Libor and Vidal, two wealthy friends, had an ongoing argument. Did wealth come mainly from good luck or hard work?

2.   "Luck is most important," declared Libor. He had become a wealthy entrepreneur after winning money in a contest.

3.   "No, work hard and plan ahead—that's the way to wealth," Vidal replied. "'No pain, no gain' is what I always say." He had toiled, saved, and invested wisely, and now owned a vast farm.

4.   The friends decided to test their beliefs. One day, on the way to sell merchandise, they encountered Pedro, a poor miller who barely earned enough to feed his family. They gave Pedro 100 pesos to use as he pleased.

5.   Pedro immediately bought meat for his family, but on his way home, a hawk swooped down to steal the meat. Pedro clutched the food, and the hawk flew off with a bag containing the remainder of the money.

Reread and use the prompts to take notes in the text.

Circle what Libor and Vidal say about wealth. Underline clues that show why Libor and Vidal choose Pedro to test their argument. Write the reason here:

_____

_____

COLLABORATE

Reread paragraphs 4–6. Draw a box around what happens to the money that was given to Pedro? Talk with a partner about Pedro's situation. Use text evidence to support your discussion and write your response below.

_____

_____

1   Discouraged, Pedro gave the lead weight to a fisherman, who in exchange gave Pedro the first fish he caught. When Pedro's wife cut open the fish to clean it, she found a diamond in its stomach, which Pedro sold for a large sum. He used the money to expand his mill. Working harder than ever, he soon found himself milling grain for all the farmers in the area.

2   One year later, Libor and Vidal saw how prosperous Pedro had become. When the miller told them about the diamond, Libor nodded. "You became wealthy through luck."

3   "But if I hadn't worked every day from dawn until dusk, I could have lost everything," said Pedro.

4   Vidal nodded. "Yes, wealth results from hard work and planning."

5   In the end, the two men could never agree about the true key to wealth.

Reread paragraph 1. Draw a box around the details that show how Pedro became wealthy through good luck. Underline the details that show how he became wealthy through hard work.

COLLABORATE

Reread paragraphs 2–4. Talk about Pedro's path to success. What is the author saying about how Pedro became wealthy?

Use your annotations to support your response.

_____

_____

_____

_____

_____

? **How does the author use the folktale characters to teach a lesson?**

COLLABORATE

Talk About It Reread the excerpts on pages 190 and 191. With a partner, discuss why the author doesn't specify the "true key to wealth."

Cite Text Evidence What clues show the true key to wealth for Pedro? Write text evidence in the web below.

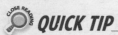
QUICK TIP

When I reread, I can think about how the author uses characters in a folktale to teach a lesson.

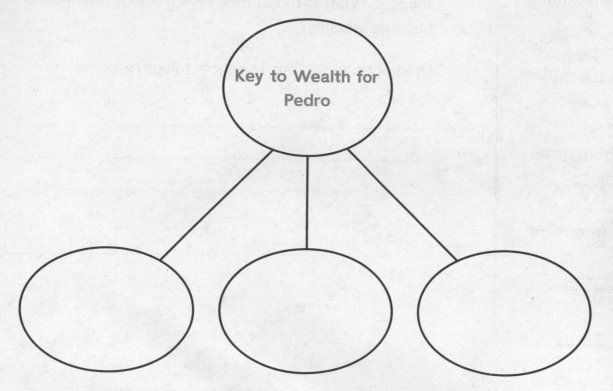

Key to Wealth for Pedro

Write The author uses the folktale characters to teach a lesson by _____

_____

_____

How does the writer use words and phrases in the rhyme and how is it similar to the way the authors in *The Big Picture of Economics* and "The Miller's Good Luck" talk about money to help you understand the role it plays?

COLLABORATE

Talk About It Read the rhyme. Talk with a partner about how the author describes money.

Cite Text Evidence Underline the line that tells you what the song will be about. Draw a box around the lines that tell you what the king is doing and where he is. Circle phrases that describe how money helps them live.

Write The rhyme and selections I read this week help me understand the role of money by _____

_____

_____

_____

_____

_____

Studiohio

QUICK TIP

I can use how the author describes the role of money to help me compare this rhyme to the selections I read this week.

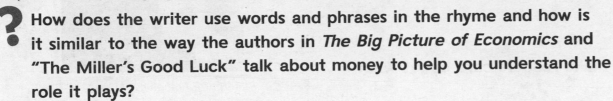

Sing a Song of Sixpence

At the edge of the tide
Sing a song of sixpence,
A pocket full of rye,
Four and twenty blackbirds
Baked in a pie.

When the pie was opened
The birds began to sing—
Wasn't that a dainty dish
To set before the king?

The king was in the counting-house
Counting out his money,
The queen was in the parlor
Eating bread and honey.

Birdfoot's Grampa

? How does the poet's use of imagery make readers care about what happens to the toads?

Talk About It Reread stanza 3 on page 535. Talk with a partner about what you visualize in this last stanza.

Cite Text Evidence Identify words and phrases used by the poet to paint a picture of Grampa saving the toads. What do these words and phrases say about Grampa's hands and the toads? Write text evidence.

Sensory Language	Why is this effective?

Write The poet's use of imagery makes readers care about what happens to the toads by _____

_____

Literature Anthology:
pages 534–536

Tip of the Week

When I **reread**, I can think about how the poet describes characters and events. I look for specific words the poet uses to create an image.

Grace

Michi B./Moment/Getty Images

My Chinatown

? How does the poet's description of the sewing machine help you understand the speaker's relationship with her mother?

Talk About It With a partner, reread "My Chinatown." Turn to your partner and talk about why the speaker would compare her mother's work on the sewing machine to a lullaby.

Cite Text Evidence Explain how the poet's description of the sewing machine helps you understand how the speaker feels about her mother's work. Is the sewing machine comforting or upsetting? Write text evidence in the web.

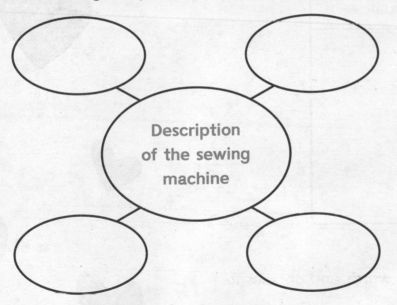

Description of the sewing machine

Write The poet's description of the sewing machine helps me understand _____

_____

_____

QUICK TIP

When I reread, I look for specific words the author uses to describe the sewing machine. Then I think about what these words tell me about the speaker and her mother.

Your Turn

How do the poets use imagery to communicate how the things people do shape who they are?

Use these sentence frames to organize your text evidence.

The poets use words and phrases to . . .

They use sensory language to create imagery so that I can . . .

This helps me understand that people are . . .

Go Digital!
Write your response online.

Growing Up

? In the poem "Growing Up," how does the poet use words and phrases to help you understand the poem's message?

COLLABORATE

Talk About It Reread "Growing Up" on page 538. Talk with a partner about how you know who is talking in the poem.

Cite Text Evidence What words and phrases help you know what the speaker in the poem is like? Write text evidence in the chart.

Text Evidence	What I Visualize

Write I understand the message because the poet uses words and phrases to

_____

_____

CLOSE READING

QUICK TIP

When I reread, I can use the poet's words and phrases to help me understand what the poem's message is.

My People

? How does Langston Hughes use comparisons to communicate a message?

Talk About It Reread "My People" on page 539. Talk to a partner about what you visualize using the poet's comparisons.

Cite Text Evidence What strong comparisons does the poet make? What is the poet saying about all of these things? Write text evidence in the chart.

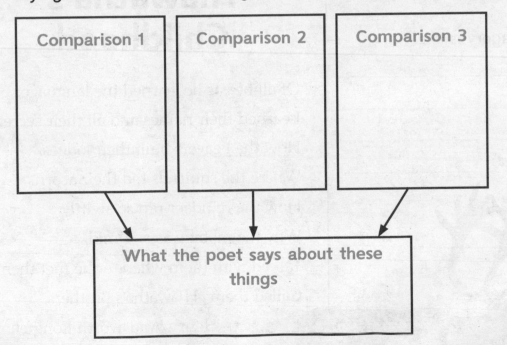

Comparison 1	Comparison 2	Comparison 3

What the poet says about these things

Write The poet uses comparisons to communicate a message about _____

_____

When I reread, I pay attention to the way the poet uses figurative language. This helps me understand the poem's message.

? How does Henry Wadsworth Longfellow help you visualize what influenced Hiawatha's life and how is it similar to the way the poets help you picture what influences the people in the poems you read this week?

COLLABORATE

Talk About It Read "Hiawatha's Childhood." Talk with a partner about what Hiawatha did.

Cite Text Evidence Underline words and phrases that show Hiawatha's actions. Circle how you know how Hiawatha felt about the animals.

Write Henry Wadsworth Longfellow's use of imagery is like _____

_____

_____

_____

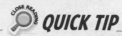

QUICK TIP

I see words and phrases that describe what shaped Hiawatha's personality. This will help me compare "Hiawatha's Childhood" to the other poems I read this week.

Hiawatha's Childhood

Of all beasts he learned the language,
Learned their names and all their secrets,
How the beavers built their lodges,
Where the squirrels hid their acorns,
How the reindeer ran so swiftly,
Why the rabbit was so timid,
Talked with them whene'er he met them,
Called them "Hiawatha's Brothers."

— Henry Wadsworth Longfellow

Design Pics/Jason Witherspoon